SO YOU'RE A LITTLE SAD, SO WHAT?

nice things to say to yourself on bad days and other essays

ALICIA TOBIN

ROBIN'S EGG BOOKS
an imprint of
ARSENAL PULP PRESS
VANCOUVER

SO YOU'RE A LITTLE SAD, SO WHAT?

Published in the United States of America in 2020

ROBIN'S EGG BOOKS is an imprint of
ARSENAL PULP PRESS
Suite 202 – 211 East Georgia St.
Vancouver, BC V6A 1Z6
Canada
arsenalpulp.com

The publisher gratefully acknowledges the support of the Canada Council for the Arts and the British Columbia Arts Council for its publishing program, and the Government of Canada, and the Government of British Columbia (through the Book Publishing Tax Credit Program), for its publishing activities.

Arsenal Pulp Press acknowledges the xʷməθkʷəy̓əm (Musqueam), Sḵwx̱wú7mesh (Squamish), and səl̓ilwətaʔɬ (Tsleil-Waututh) Nations, speakers of Hul'q'umi'num'/Halq'eméylem/hənq̓əminəm̓ and custodians of the traditional, ancestral, and unceded territories where our office is located. We pay respect to their histories, traditions, and continuous living cultures and commit to accountability, respectful relations, and friendship.

Cover and text design by Oliver McPartlin
Edited by Charles Demers
Copy edited by Kimmy Beach and Shirarose Wilensky
Proofread by Jaiden Dembo and Alison Strobel

Printed and bound in Canada

Library and Archives Canada Cataloguing in Publication:
Title: So you're a little sad, so what? : nice things to say to yourself on bad days and other essays / Alicia Tobin.
Names: Tobin, Alicia, 1975– author.
Identifiers: Canadiana (print) 20190131209 | Canadiana (ebook) 20190131217 | ISBN 9781551527871 (softcover) | ISBN 9781551527888 (HTML)
Subjects: CSH: Canadian essays (English)
Classification: LCC PS8639.O25 S69 2019 | DDC C814/.6—dc23

I dedicate this book to my family and my friends—
YOU KNOW WHO YOU ARE—(for your constant
love and support, which gets me through
all kinds of days).

Thank you to Charlie Demers and everyone at
Arsenal Pulp Press for your kindness and guidance
during the writing of this book.

CONTENTS

FOREWORD

Behold, reader, the birth of a new literary genre: goofball melancholia. You are a bit (or a lot) sad, and Alicia Tobin is a bit (or a lot) sad, but she is also sensitive and funny (not that I'm saying you aren't), and as you each negotiate a world filled with shitty jobs, shitty housing markets, the occasional shitty person, injured pets, injured egos, and frustrated ambitions, two of the only things you can count on to get you through are loved ones and good jokes. Also, large plates of baked goods.

For many decades, posh Old Money people have cultivated what is called the mid-Atlantic accent, building an identity that is halfway between New York and London. I think one of the reasons I've always felt connected to Alicia is that, like me, her whole sensibility is mid-whatever-is-exactly-in-between-Vancouver-and-Montreal (she has split her life so far evenly between the two cities; I was raised by a Québécois dad on the coast of the Pacific). The internet tells me that the spot exactly in between Vancouver and Montreal is Bismarck, North Dakota, but it isn't: it's Alicia Tobin's brain. That means she knows what it feels like to do a cleanse but can also tell Du Maurier smoke from that of an inferior brand. She has felt the calm of Savasana but also knows how to dress. An old friend of mine of mixed Jewish and French Canadian heritage used to identify as a kosher poutine, and in that spirit, I propose that Alicia is a gluten-free tourtière.

I remember well when Alicia first came onto the Vancouver comedy scene. It isn't particularly rare for a beautiful person to start doing comedy, but Alicia was something of a special case. It's not that her beauty wasn't remarked upon (as you'll read in these pages, it was—sometimes piggishly), but that it felt somehow less important than the fact that she was so frigging *elegant*. My wife said she looked like an Old Hollywood movie star (as in, a star from Old Hollywood, not a Hollywood star who is old). Funny and beautiful happens all the time, but funny and elegant is almost impossible to pull off. In fact, modern comedy was born when a man with patches on the bum of his trousers threw a pie at the best-dressed lady in the room. Comedically, Alicia was not only both the pie-thrower *and* the well-dressed lady, but she also baked the pie (along with a small rice-flour alternative for a celiac friend). And when she got hit in the face with the pie, she took the plate into another room and ate the filling to soothe her tender feelings.

Allow me to make this all about me for a moment, if you will: my mother was unable to work from the time I was five, and died when I was ten, so, economically speaking, I was raised by my dad alone, a widower who worked as a teacher. When you're raised by a single-parent teacher, you live in the no man's land of class hierarchy: put in the broadest, crudest terms possible, you have working-class money and upper-middle-class culture. As it happens, my dad was also a gay man (still is!) who shared with his sons a deep love of beauty and style. I'm sorry that this particular autobiographical detail aligns so closely with hurtful stereotypes; I'm certain that some guys' gay dads taught them how to tighten a fan belt and field dress a deer. Mine didn't.

All of this is to say that when you grow up the way I did, the only people around whom you feel entirely at ease are those who know of and long for the finer things in life but also can't afford them. As you are about to discover while reading this book, Alicia is one of those people: someone who knows precisely the most glamorous and sophisticated way to decorate the apartment she's being evicted from. She's the cultural equivalent of a chinchilla stole in a thrift store—though, to paraphrase English Canada's greatest troubadours, not a real mink stole; that's cruel.

That's why I'm so proud to present Alicia Tobin's first book of essays—this one, the one in your hand and/or hands. It is a piece of working-class elegance. Bread and roses, for someone who bloats from yeast and gets hay fever from flowers. I'm pretty sad, and pretty funny, which is why Alicia's work has always landed so hard with me—as it has with thousands of podcast listeners, comedy crowds, and comedians. She is effortlessly hilarious, without the plausible deniability of pain provided by irony. She has an oozy, gooey heart that at first you think must be pie filling, then no, it's a heart, then pie filling, then a heart ...

So? You're a little sad. So what? Read this.

Charles Demers
Robin's Egg Books Editor & Emotional Eater

VELCRO

I was excited about grade four because I had new shoes, cool shoes. I always had good leather shoes, whereas the average child had sneakers, but nothing says a child can't be active and play in a pair of good leather shoes! (If the year is 1940.) My mother dressed my brother and me very well, in "real" fabrics, like cotton and wool, and our private-school uniforms were crisp and clean for the first day of school each year. Sadly, we didn't go to a private school. We went to a Protestant public school in Pointe-Claire, Quebec.

The annual late-August hunt for shoes was so simple: my mother would take me to Buster Brown for a new pair of exactly the same shoes I had been wearing since preschool: navy leather Mary Janes with a gummy sole. The cool thing about those shoes was that the sole had little train wheels on them. That's cool, right? I would look around the shop at the new shoes, the fun shoes, and dream of wearing something that might help me fit in with the other kids. But I stayed silent as the clerk fit my feet with my practical, well-made shoes.

My mother would loudly explain that I had wide feet "like her father's," and that it was very difficult "to find proper shoes for her wide feet." She would shout out similar facts about my body when buying pants, which was impossible because "she has a very long body but short legs AND a very short inseam," and I would close my eyes, my cheeks burning with shame over my little iguana body and my mother's ability to point out things that were wrong with me that I couldn't possibly change.

I don't know, maybe I'd already had a good dose of sugar and food colouring that day when we went to the shoe store and I wandered over and placed my small summer-tanned hand on a pair of light blue suede North Star runners with Velcro straps. Velcro was new, a space-age invention, and something I can say everyone was very excited about. I mean, Brian Mulroney was the prime minister, so we had to look to something for hope. These shoes were technically leather, and they were technically blue leather, and I let my hand rest on them and looked over at my mother, using my good eye, not my lazy eye, and hoped she could feel me looking at her with my most powerful eye.

"Do you like those?" she asked in her smoky voice.

"Yes," I said, my heart skipping a beat.

She asked the clerk if they made the sneakers in wide, and he said no.

"Well, why don't you try them?" she said.

And I did. And they were too tight, but when my mom reached down to see where my toes were, I pulled them back, just a bit.

"Do you promise to wear them, Alicia?"

I did. And that was the first time I chose something just for me, and the beginning of a long history of lying to my mother about shoes fitting and a variety of other things, like how many cookies I had eaten and how long my torso really is. Maybe it isn't how long my torso is or isn't, maybe it's how many cigarettes you smoked when you were pregnant, which in 1975, was quite a lot, so who knows why my torso is long or short, right, Mom?

I put the North Stars beside my bed and waited for the first day of school. I didn't sleep much as a child, so it comforted me to have them beside my bed to help quell my anxiety. I didn't have any close friends at school. Olaf, my dear friend who didn't laugh at my eye patch, transferred to a private school over the summer, after he was caught doing an "underpants dance" he had been coerced into by some kids who had the advantage of being the bullies and not the bullied. Olaf's stern father was mortified and removed his sweet child from public school, and we never saw each other again. Olaf, if you are reading this, I hope you are so rich!

My new shoes were my new-found confidence. I started to look forward to school and counted the days to our fourth-grade debut. The year before, I wasn't as confident. I had to wear an eye patch to school each day, and because of a short-lived attempt by my parents to save a bit of money, instead of a bandage-style patch, I wore a real eye patch, like a tiny pirate, and shiver me timbers, that was an unpopular look. Perhaps if I wasn't already a sensitive and self-conscious child, I would have handled the eye patch better. But I had a tantrum whenever my parents tried to get me to socialize with other kids, and the eye patch made it so much worse. I remember getting to the doorway of my first and only Brownies meeting and screaming until my mother took me home. I know now that this was a panic attack, but I was so small, and my torso so long, that it was hard to tell.

My parents tried, but who puts a kid with one good eye in basketball camp? Or soccer? Or piano? I just wanted to draw and hang out with my dog, or my two summer friends who didn't go to the same school as I did.

I was shy, but I also wanted to be heard, and this would come out in terrible ways, with me often breaking into an inappropriate joke I had heard on one of my parents' many comedy albums. Or when we had a group project to make Easter puppets, mine was the only Mary Magdalene in the show. When other children asked who the puppet was, I would say, "Mary MAGDALENE."

And they would say, "Oh, Jesus's mother?"

And I would say, "NO SHE WAS A PROSTITUTE AND JESUS'S FRIEND SHE IS THE OTHER MARY IN THE BIBLE SHEESH" and turn my good eye back to my weird puppet.

Grade four was going to be better. I had two Cabbage Patch Kids now, which was quite a bit of social clout, and I didn't have to wear my eye patch at school anymore, just my thick glasses, so progress was happening style-wise. I was looking forward to gym class—I had my new sneakers, and with my glasses, I could see a wayward ball headed towards my curly noggin and bat it away with my normal-sized arms. Life. Was. Looking. Up!

The first gym class of the year was a perfect chance to show off my new shoes. I sat down and pushed my feet into them and sharp pains shot up my toes. Perfect fit! I gingerly pulled the Velcro straps closed. I joined the circle of other children waiting to see what our gym teacher, Mr Sparkle (name changed out of deep respect for a great teacher) had planned for us today. I eyed the ropes and thought this would be the year I would climb to the top. Then I readjusted my Velcro straps, for two reasons: I wanted to give my wide feet a breath of fresh air, and I wanted to alert my peers to the new cool kid in town. As I pulled back the strap again to get the fit just right, Mr Sparkle stopped speaking, turned to me, and asked if I was done interrupting him. At first, I thought I had said out loud the bit about how everyone should take note of my new shoes, but he meant the sound of the Velcro. Mr Sparkle hated Velcro with every fibre of his sinewy gym-teacher body. Some of the other children looked at me sympathetically, and others who were perched to readjust their own Velcro shoes pulled away in newly cautious horror. I looked down at my lovely shoes, my shoes that would change my world, and fought back tears. Would I never get anything right?

Mr Sparkle made a rule that we could not play with our shoes during class, that sneakers are not toys, and anyway, what was so wrong with shoes with laces? His face was turning red; his hands trembled. For many of the children, this was the first time a teacher had yelled at them. Not an adult, though. It was the 1980s and parents yelled constantly at their children, but not a trusted and truly beloved adult like Mr Sparkle.

I looked at my shoes. My feet ached. You only got one pair of sneakers each year and you had to make them last. I knew we couldn't afford another pair, and I was already waiting out the weeks until I could convince my mom that my feet had grown a full size and I needed a new pair. I worried at the edges of the Velcro straps and ached to hear the satisfying crunch. Concentrating as hard as I could not to touch my shoes, I barely heard the invitation to learn gymnastics from the two gym teachers after school each Tuesday and Thursday. I perked up. Cool girls did gymnastics. I could be a cool kid, too? And it was free. I wouldn't have to ask my parents to pay for it, which was perfect, as I had kind of blown it with ballet lessons when my parents learned quickly that I had only wanted the ballet outfit and not the experience of learning ballet, and certainly not the company of my peers. Free was exactly the price they would be willing to pay.

I showed up at the gym after school on Tuesday. Mr Sparkle patiently helped all of us navigate the springboard, explained the pommel horse, and asked if we thought we should put on an event for the parents at the end of the semester. We all agreed. There is something so without risk during childhood that we never get back as adults.

We had to choose one area of the gym we felt really passionate about. I loved to dance, so I chose the highest art of rhythmic gymnastics: the mesmerizing ribbon dance! I felt so cool as I practised alone on the mat, my red ribbon floating above the simple but intense dance moves I made up on the spot. A cartwheel? Sure! A jump? You bet! A somersault? Ouch! I practised my heart out. At home at night I listened to all my cassettes (one, I had one) and chose my song for the big night.

When I gave the tape to Mr Sparkle, positioned myself on the mat, ribbon in hand, and told him to press play, the sweet warble of Tina Turner singing "Private Dancer" filled the gymnasium. I felt so cool. I spun, I cartwheeled, I moved my little body in time to the lyrics, which I didn't understand at all.

After only a few lines, Mr Sparkle pulled the tape out and said, "Alicia, you can't dance to this song!"

I felt like crying. I'd really connected with that song: I was being a PRIVATE DANCER, just for the audience, no one else was dancing with me! It was perfect.

"Why?"

"Ask your mother," he barked, and handed me back the tape.

With the performance just a few weeks away I had to find new music, fast. Back in the day, you had to wait for a good song to play on the radio, and then press play and record at the exact right time on your tape deck to record it. Mr Sparkle had suggested the Beatles and asked if I had a tape of their tried-and-true ribbon dance songs. I practised to "Eleanor Rigby," which made for the saddest ribbon dance on earth. Mr Sparkle wasn't happy. "Choose something fun!" he urged.

I was running out of options.

I tried "Billie Jean" by Michael Jackson, another hard no.

"Roxanne" by the Police? Nope.

Mr Sparkle never told me why I couldn't use these songs, and I never asked.

Finally, we agreed on another Beatles song: "A Hard Day's Night." Perfect. Ribbon. Dance. Song?

The night before the performance, I started to have second thoughts about the tune. It just felt so uncool. As that wonderful childhood innocence and lack of self-consciousness started putting on its jacket and giving me a "hang loose" salute, I started to worry that the audience wouldn't like it, and I didn't sleep that night.

That afternoon, I waited my turn at the lunchtime show. My parents were in the audience, looking nervous (they always looked nervous for me).

I gently pulled off my shoes—Mr Sparkle tensed as he heard the Velcro crack—walked over to the stereo, and handed him my music. There was a round of applause, and I nodded to Mr Sparkle to press play.

Madonna's voice came over the speakers and I danced. I ribonned! I spun, I cartwheeled, I somersaulted, as Madge sang, her lyrics so perfectly capturing the exhilaration of this shiny new feeling, as for the very first time, with my heart beating—

The music stopped.

I looked over at Mr Sparkle; he was as white as a ghost. I didn't know what to do. I just kept dancing and singing "Like a Virgin" as loud as I could until I ran out of dance moves or breath, I'm not sure. I bowed, waved, and ran back to my classmates.

Mr Sparkle couldn't look at me, but I didn't know why.

At home that night, my mom explained to me what a virgin was, what a private dance was, and what the deal was with Billie Jean.

Next gym class I wore new shoes, with laces, and kept my head down. My cheeks burned to think about how my innocent dance was not innocent at all anymore.

At some point, Mr Sparkle went on leave. There were rumours that he'd had a nervous breakdown, but I think that was just what people said when someone needed a break from children. Still, I always wondered: Was it the Velcro, or was it Madonna?

RACCOON HANDS

I was watching the CBC one night and a documentary about raccoons came on, so I said quietly to myself, "Holy shit, finally some programming for me!"

Basically, all I ever want is news about animals and for someone to love me unconditionally. So I grabbed my couch with my butt, which is hard because I have no butt. At first, I slid off onto the floor, and then I pulled myself back up and settled in for some serious raccoon school.

Did you know that raccoons have collapsible spines? Can you imagine how much easier getting into a wet bathing suit would be, or going along with bad ideas at work? Or reaching something that is pushed way back under the couch, but you don't want to move the couch because moving the couch stirs up too many emotions? Oh, you don't get stressed out by moving the couch? Okay, fine. Wait, for real? But once you see all the dirty dirt under there, you can't just put the couch back and knowingly go on with your day, can you? And feel like a person who is doing okay in life and has things under control?

Anyway, a collapsible spine allows raccoons to sneak into a garage through a tiny space between the door and the frame, to have a place to give birth to a litter of the cutest cubs. Raccoons are actually very tidy animals. They use only one spot to go to the bathroom, away from their nest, and probably on your deck. Careful when cleaning it up; their poop contains a potentially harmful parasite. Pretty neat, eh? Not yet? Okay, hang tight!

Not only do raccoons have collapsible spines and deadly poop, but they also have amazing hands. Paws? Haws. Hand-paws. Oof, did I just have a stroke? Raccoons have sensory nubs similar to taste buds in their hand-paws that allow them to know, just by touch, if something is food. So, in a way, when they are touching something, they are also tasting it. That means you could touch all the chocolates (when no one is looking; no one needs to know your private business) and determine which one is the orange cream and eat all the other ones first, until shamefully eating that one, too. It also basically means that whenever a raccoon gives another raccoon a hand job, it's also giving them a blow job! At least, this was what the CBC led me to believe, and the Queen of England owns the CBC, so yeah.

I am a big fan of raccoons, but at the same time, I will consider abandoning my apartment if I get home at night and one is in my yard. A raccoon is a ninja star covered in fur, so, little raccoon, this place is yours now. Please enjoy my mid-century furniture and my perpetual container of expired spring mix in the crisper drawer—or as I call it, the fridge coffin.

I take offence to people calling raccoons trash pandas. It's inaccurate and disrespectful. Not to mention, I have never been very interested in pandas, except that time a panda mauled someone for trying to spoon with it at the zoo in the middle of the night, which I understand—spooning must be consensual, and pandas probably have to work even harder to create boundaries because they are so tired all the time. People are more like trash pandas, always with the garbage we are. Making garbage, piling it up, and being lazy about doing anything about it or our place in the world. Then we gaslight animals trying to survive in a hostile takeover of their habitat. We poison them, we trap them, and we kill them for being who they are, all because we don't care. I could say we don't understand them or we feel threatened by them, but the truth is we actively choose not to care.

Take, for example, Toronto—a large Canadian city where they really disrespect raccoons. A few years ago, a dead raccoon was found on the sidewalk and when the city didn't respond to numerous requests to remove the animal, fancy financiers, hedge fund managers, comedians who actually make money doing comedy, and celebrity florists thought it would be funny to make a joke of a helpless animal who died in the middle of a cruel city. They made a fake memorial and—I have to be honest—at first, I thought it was real because the raccoon deserved some kind words and well wishes as his spirit was no doubt ushered into a heaven that was peaceful, lush, and devoid of streets or cars.

Sometimes we may not feel like we have enough caring to extend to animals, especially animals other than cats and dogs that weren't bred to be companions. If we did care, though, we would learn that raccoons are very smart and very good parents (they don't let their cubs see them smoke weed for sure, and they definitely don't feed them yogourt tubes, unless they find one in the garbage and they make an exception). It isn't so hard to respect them, and even appreciate them, once you get to know how special they are.

On a morning walk with my dog, as the sun was rising over my East Vancouver neighbourhood, I came across the body of a raccoon cub, killed by a car on Fraser Street. I felt woozy as the dog pulled on his leash to get closer. The cub's beautiful coat moved softly in the wind, and I could see that one of his eyes had been dislodged and now rested on his cheek. It seemed so terribly unfair that such a smart animal would die because of a stupid car.

I started to walk away and then saw movement. As I turned back towards the raccoon, his family rushed out of the alley and each touched him gently, making soft noises, as if saying goodbye in a language we do not understand. And then they cautiously crossed Fraser Street, heads low on purpose-filled bodies. In that morning light, I was reminded that raccoons are more like us than not but with much, much better fur. And deserving of understanding, respect, and a better name than Trash Panda.

SECRET FOOD

Last night I walked to the corner store. I had planned on buying some baked goods, but the credit card machine was down at the nice bakery, so I left my pecan pie and mint brownie at the cash. What was I going to do? *It's fine. I will be fine.* I ate something dinner-like for dinner instead of pastries and tried not to think about sugar. But at 6:30 I was in the corner store, dog in tow, buying Snickers bars and gummy bears, enough for a two-hour movie that would actually last me a few minutes into a walk with the dog. I tucked my drugs, I mean treats, into my pocket and walked out after acting totally normal as best I could but thinking about how in a few moments I would have the sweet relief this candy would bring me. I felt good about this purchase, but in the past I didn't always.

I have been at a similar counter, at a similar place, making the same kind of purchase, for almost forty years. It is familiar but always fraught with emotion. I think deeply about what is the most I can buy without looking like I have a problem. I scan the somewhat empty shelves for favourites—which don't include fancy or fun Ritter Sports, or anything with dark chocolate because that has nowhere near the amount of sugar I like—and hope I don't have to walk out empty-handed. With my food allergies, I have to read every label to make sure a treat doesn't manifest in crushing abdominal pain. I also hope no one I know walks in. I never make these purchases at the grocery store or buy junk food at Whole Foods. I rarely eat anything like this in front of anyone. This is my secret food.

Shame always loses to desire and need, however, and I never feel judged by the candy-store man. He sees me, all the time, all day long. He may be the lotto ticket guy or the wine keeper or the smoke-shop keep, but he's always my candy man. He used to be the smoke man, the wine guy, and the candy man, but my vices have narrowed now.

I stepped out into the cold January air, peeled back the wrapper on the Snickers bar, told the dog he couldn't have any, and finished it in three bites. And then I ripped open the bag of gummies. I wondered if dogs can eat gummies and decided, no, they can't. Plus, more for me. I saw a man about my age and put the candy back into my parka pocket. I looked down and held my candy-scented breath until he passed.

You might think I have a complicated relationship with food. But this isn't food, now is it? I have a complicated relationship with feelings. Food is one of the ways I deal with my inability to deal with my feelings. I have too many feelings and not enough sweetness to deal with them.

There's a story about me taking slices of bread from the breadbox when I was very small. I don't remember the day this happened. I am sure it happened all the time, but this was the first time there was a recorded history of my "eating style." My mom was curled up on a kitchen chair on the phone, but I didn't know she was in there, and I didn't see her as I waddled into the kitchen in a droopy diaper and nothing else, opened the breadbox, pulled out a slice of bread, crammed it into my baby face, and ran back out the other side of the kitchen. Repeat. I ate half a loaf this way, my mom silently laughing at me as I poked soft slices of bread into my mouth. So I guess at about age two I had already started what would be a lifelong habit of sneaking food. I am a very charming lady with absolutely no issues! Date me?

I would always think a lot about food. I liked the way it made me feel. I couldn't eat it fast enough and could get through any meal, even Salisbury steak or meat loaf, to reach dessert. And then, hopefully, seconds of dessert. And then after dinner I would sneak back into the kitchen and slice off tiny crooked pieces of the pie or cake that was left over, until nothing remained.

At childhood birthday parties I would always try to sit beside the birthday kid, meaning I would be served cake second and most likely be done before any other child and could then raise my hand for a second helping of cake and ice cream, thirds if I was surrounded by lightweights. I mastered chewing like a shark. Bite, swallow. Most adults thought this was cute, but I can remember one birthday party where my friend's mother asked me to save some for the other children, and I burned hot with shame until the end of the party, unable to play, wondering what was wrong with me. But also, still really thinking about that second piece of cake I had not savoured because I assumed a third was on its way.

When my father or mother would give my brother and me our allowance (I worked for it, I promise), I would sit down and think about the maximum amount of candy I could buy. I wanted maximum sugar and minimum salt. We always had chips at home, so I could augment any candy-store acquisitions with the stash at the house. At that time, we lived in a small town in the West Island of Montreal that had a beautiful candy store called Generations. It was the early eighties and two Canadian dollars equalled ... a lot of candy. One full-sized chocolate bar, one package of sponge candy, a handful of wax bottles, a few cola gummies, and in the summer, a Popsicle, all of which I would eat before making it out of the parking lot. I loved sugar. I would eat lumps of brown sugar from the bag, take sips of maple syrup, and devour powdered iced tea by the spoonful, coughing through each bite. And I did this in secret. When I was sad, or scared, or anxious. It calmed me. If something happened at home or school, which was daily, I would eat something sweet. My heart would race, my stomach would hurt, and for a length of time, my brain would shut down the constant babble: *my parents are going to get divorced, I have no friends, my brother hates me.* All were facts I could fade out for a time while my body tried to cope with the influx of Red 40, corn syrup, and milk chocolate. It was truly a sweet relief.

Sweets were not villainized in my family, but being fat was. At nine or so, I started to gain weight. We had moved to another town, and I wasn't having a lot of luck integrating into a new school in a mostly French town. My parents were at each other every day, and my brother was hitting his teens full force. I had one friend, who had been part of a search party sent out to find a kid with a lazy left eye and crazy, curly hair when I got horribly lost on our first weekend in our new house. I don't know what I would have done without my friend Sherry. If you are reading this, Sherry, you are the prototype for a loyal friend.

Sherry loved food too, and we planned our lonely days around Madonna dance parties and trips to the depanneur corner store to buy treats and our parents cigarettes. Sherry's family had a cookie jar that I fed from freely. I think I ate a minimum of ten cookies every time I went over (and thought about them the entire time I wasn't eating them). Store-bought cookies were the ultimate treat. My mother baked every

Wednesday—lovely cookies and cakes—but something about these crunchy, flavourless cookies made my feelings disappear faster.

When Sherry was held back a year in school, I entered grade five without a friend. It was a turning point for my secret eating. I started stealing food. I would leave class, feeling anxious and angry and left out, and snoop through other children's lunches, pilfer a cherished treat from a lunch box or bag, and eat it in a bathroom stall. I wanted to take something from them, something sweet, that I didn't have. I think when you are small you can't imagine that any other child has unhappiness like yours, that other families are disasters. I hated those kids, with their packed lunches and store-bought treats and nice clothes and friends. This was the same year that I dressed up as an undercover-cop-disguised-as-a-prostitute for the grade five Halloween dance, so not having friends does seem pretty in line with the choices I was making. I watched a lot of grown-up TV with my only other friend at that time: my mom. I also stand by the fact that my costume, however tone-deaf, was a manifestation of the feminism I was raised with: if you were smart enough to become a leading investigator, you were still expected to be a sexy laaaaaaady!

I started to wonder at that time, too, if I would be fat. It was a fat-free time. Oh, what a time to be hungry! What a time to be a creative child who was more than what she weighed or how she looked! Everyone was running, eating boiled skinless chicken breasts, using fat-free products, and doing step classes. Meanwhile, I was sneaking off to the store every other morning before school under the guise of walking the dog to buy two chocolate bars with money I stole from my parents' pockets to deal with the anxiety of the day ahead. I would tie my dog, Prince, outside

Pierrettes (a chain of Quebec depanneurs that have been replaced by thousands of Provi-soirs) and usually buy one Crunchie bar and one Aero Peppermint bar. I would quickly eat them on the walk home, disposing of the wrappers on the way to school. If no one saw me, it didn't happen, right? My mom started to get concerned, though; I was gaining weight but apparently eating normally. She poked my belly questioningly. I hid behind the family dog in pictures, wore the same jogging suit every day until it didn't fit and was replaced by something similarly loose, and ate everything I could when no one was around. It helped so much with the yelling at home, the fear at school, the bullying and teasing I endured and handed out when Sherry wasn't around.

All I wanted was to unwrap the candy to have that first bite of calm and hide in my room with my books. I started to master shutting out the yelling in my home, the stress at school, with an equation of chocolate bars + cookies + books = feeling okay. I stopped taking the school bus after a misguided attempt to assume power by becoming the school bus monitor (I ruled like Stalin, not Gandhi—oy, especially snacks-wise—and was ousted). Too embarrassed to take the bus anymore, I started walking to school, and walking and reading a book and eating, sometimes at the same time, became my only ways of coping until the present day. I became the person who walked everywhere, read all the books for class before anyone else had, and in private, ate all the food. I was definitely laid off of a few babysitting jobs not only for being a terrible babysitter but also for eating all of the children's treats. *Oh, sorry, did you have a plan for those Fruit Roll-Ups?*

Walking helped manage so much more than eating. It gave me time to think about the day ahead, or the night that would follow after school. I started to almost sense when I would be coming home to a bad night; sometimes I could smell the cleaning products from the curb in front of my house or hear the roar of the central vacuum and knew my mother was angry. Or the house would be eerily still, and I would know my mom was in bed and wouldn't open her door today. The walk helped me stay calm and think about how to handle a life where I only had a bit of control. The food helped when something terrible was said at home or school. I had my own way of coping with my early-onset disappointment. The weight that had my mother so worried was walked off, and big muscles and a straight back came out of my soft childhood.

High school brought with it the cultural shame associated with overeating and bodies that were anything but skinny. I started to worry about my weight and skipped lunches because I felt anxious eating around other kids. I would still eat secretly, but I started to feel guilty and ashamed. I would wake up in the middle of the night to eat after a day of thinking about food. Eating helped me sleep a few hours, knocking me out, until I had to crawl out of bed for another day of hoping it would be better. Often still stopping by the corner store for a chocolate bar on the way to school and feeling the rush of the sugar hitting my system, and the numbness, as I walked through the doors for another day of high school horse shit. After school I would eat so much, feel sick, wait for the feeling to subside, repeat. Being numb, feeling sick—both better than hearing the constant internal monologue about how ugly I was, how stupid. Just a few minutes of reprieve from the facts of life: school was an awful and constant assault on the spirit, filled with sexual harassment and groping, cliques, gateway drugs, and chaos. Home was scary. Hello, donuts!

When I moved to Montreal from the suburbs the summer I turned eighteen, I faced real food insecurity for the first time. I survived on tins of soup, cheap diner meals, snacks provided by kind and maternal co-workers, and day-old baked goods. On payday I would buy a cake and eat it alone, and go to bed alone, and cry. My anxiety was unchecked. I actually didn't know that I was having anxiety attacks. I just thought I was shy and overwhelmed, and I had only a few friends who often didn't have much time to drag me out of my little apartment and explain me to their other friends. I was working full time and barely making enough for rent and bills. I would force myself to sit in the Atwater shopping mall for a few minutes, breathing hard, feeling scared. I had no support system, no higher education, and no idea what the fuck I was meant to be doing. If I made it through the mall experience, I would allow myself to stock up on chocolate bars at the dollar store and retreat to my apartment. This continued until I made a few friends in my building and at work and started drinking socially to cope with my fear and deep feelings of inadequacy. My new friends delighted in my love of sugar, and I felt comfortable eating around them. Sometimes they would roll fat joints while I unwrapped one of three Cadbury Creme Eggs. No one thought badly of me. They thought it was cute. I started to think it was pretty cute, too. My first real boyfriend woke up one night and I was quietly eating a massive Easter egg in bed. This was who I was.

In my early twenties I started reading about food and teaching myself to cook. I never lost my abject love of sugar, but a new world opened up to me. Montreal is filled with good restaurants, affordable adventures for kids like me who couldn't afford to travel, and every neighbourhood had meals that filled my heart. I started to care about food in a deeper way.

Food didn't have to come in a candy shape, or even be candy! I started to share food and make food and learn about myself through this connection to new people, new friends, and new communities. I learned to make food that I liked and had people in my home and could eat around them and talk about life. I had a life. I started to wonder about how the food I ate made me feel. But I never asked how my feelings made me eat.

My feelings are something I am better at processing these days, but I now look at food differently. I don't feel ashamed about eating like I did when I was younger. I feel ashamed that I didn't love my body more. I feel ashamed that I bought into fat shaming and body shaming and didn't let life be more than that in so many ways. I feel sad that I didn't know as a child what was wrong, that I was anxious and scared, and gummy worms made me feel better. And I am happy that now I can enjoy my Snickers bar in the cold night and have a moment of silence within.

RETAIL

It is just past noon on a Friday in Vancouver when I muster up the nerve to buy a personal shaver at the big pharmacy/electronics/beauty/kitchen appliance store. I love this place. I can buy a vacuum, a box of tampons, and a lottery ticket all under one roof. It's basically heaven on earth as I know it.

I decide on a razor and head to the cosmetics counter nearby to pay for my new thing that I surely will never use after using it once and cutting myself badly. I gently place the product on the counter and make soft eye contact in the direction of the woman working in the area as she putters around a nail polish display. She walks behind the till and I smile at her.

She says, "May I help you?" But it isn't a question, more of an accusation, really, to which the answer is obviously: *No, I am helpless. Just look at me—I dress like a four-year-old sailor, I am definitely going to eat a piece of birthday cake for lunch, and in my pocket is a small plastic shark.*

The woman ignores the box by her cash register. I feel as though I am looking in a mirror but seeing myself at the age of sixty-five or so. She is wearing a black skirt suit, her thick silver hair shimmers, and across her lips is a shadow of red lipstick she applied this morning. She is annoyed with me. I am not sure if it is because she is focused on cleaning or I have done something wrong. Her hand has not moved to scan the razor.

I say, "Hi, I would like to buy this."

Her hand still does not move, but her eyes look at the box with disdain and then back up at me, her gaze unchanged. She hisses, "Would you like to buy anything from this department?"

Well, she just fucked with the wrong person. The razor aisle is seemingly in this department, this empty department, and definitely belongs to the same shitty intent of the cosmetics department, where I feel the constant and chronic pressure of beauty standards to keep my body hair at zero-fun levels of tame. The whole store is seemingly set up so that most of the purchases women make can be made less stressful at the beauty counter: feminine hygiene, hair removal, makeup, hair care, hand and foot care, jewellery, and a variety of other crap we don't really need but are made to feel we need can be paid for easily at the always-empty and peaceful cosmetics till. I guess we need feminine hygiene products. Some of them. Most of them? You know what I mean.

I say, calmly, "I thought this was from this department" (translation: *I just want to shave my private area so I can go to the gym and sit in the sauna and not traumatize anyone who might think Burt Reynolds's toupée is in my bathing suit zone*).

She says, "No," and before she can say her next weird line, I pull the box back and hear myself yelling, "Oh, I get it." I am not interested in playing into whatever is going on here.

She scrambles to recover her customer service hat, but it's too late; the wind of yelling has blown it into the candy aisle.

"I get it, no problem, I see what is going on here," I say, and take my dumb, stupid pink razor to the general till and pay and walk out.

I am not going to complain about the terrible service for a few reasons. One is the woman's age. I find it upsetting that someone at retirement age will probably never retire. I don't know her story, but the story I make up is that she has always worked in retail and will until the day she dies (which is punishment enough). Two, I relate really strongly to what happened from her side as well. She's trying to have a sense of control over her day and her department (it probably never happens), plus some dignity and respect (that probably never happens, either). Three, I have been shitty, too, to customers who happened to need service when I was fresh out of the ability. And the fourth reason is that she really did look like what I would have ended up looking like if I hadn't decided to get out of retail at thirty-seven. I worked in retail for almost twenty years, before hanging up my permanent smile and enthusiasm for customer service, along with feet that stood thousands of hours waiting on people, hands that folded T-shirts and pinned hems, and a brain that tried not to implode every day from the rudeness and entitlement of so many people.

I had always thought the kids in high school and CEGEP technical college who had part-time jobs in retail were very cool. Especially if they sold clothes or makeup, two areas of consumerism that I lived for. I didn't think anyone at the Gap would want me, so I stuck to babysitting and warehouse jobs, until one day, I was sitting in the Place Ville Marie shopping complex with my friend, eating ice cream from Laura Secord, a Canadian chocolate institution, when she said that working at a place like Laura Secord would be perfect, because we wouldn't have to buy any clothes to work there. Most stores that hired young people were clothing stores, and those stores ran a bit of a racket whereby they required the staff to wear the clothes they sold. Sure, you would get the clothes at a discount, but it was basically a uniform you had to pay for yourself, and in most places in Canada if you are required to wear a uniform, the employer must provide it and have it laundered for you. We eyed the chocolate store uniform: white shirt, black pants, and a green apron embroidered with the fine features of Laura Secord, Canadian heroine of the War of 1812 who stole all the chocolate from the American soldiers, so they were too sad to fight the British. These are facts, no need to check.

Anyway, there was a little sign in the window in French, indicating they were hiring part-time workers for the Easter rush. We applied, and we were interviewed on the spot and hired. I was seventeen and had never had a job interacting with the public. But I had a lot of experience eating too much chocolate, so I figured I would find my feet.

My first day at the store, wearing my faded green apron, was exciting. There were so many rules, and I love rules! It is so nice to know exactly what is expected of you instead of constantly guessing. Most of the staff were in their mid-fifties and took me under their wing, patiently showing me how to scoop ice cream (harder than it looks) and work the cash register. I was in charge of keeping the store stocked with cream eggs, hard candy, Easter bunnies, and the individual chocolates in the display case. The stock was kept in a storage room in the bowels of the shopping centre, to which I would wander periodically during the day with a list of products to find. The larger items—the chocolate bars, bunnies, and eggs—were easy to find, but the small chocolates were really challenging. Often, I would have to eat three or four of each flavour to be sure they were the right ones, before returning to the store with my dolly loaded with bright foiled treats and my stomach aching from testing so many chocolates. I found out later that the names of the chocolates were written on the boxes; I never thought to check.

When one of the regular staff needed a break, I would be put on cash or ice-cream duty, and this was when the maternal hens of Laura Secord turned into real cocks. I wasn't gifted at reaching down into a mostly empty tub and scooping out hard ice cream with a cold wet scoop. The women who worked with me had been at that location for at least a decade and didn't think I had what it took to be a full-time employee. I started to get dirty looks and deep sighs when I arrived at work. When the manager (who would shortly thereafter be caught taking a full retail-sized tub of ice cream home without paying) told me after just over a month that I wasn't being hired permanently, I felt so embarrassed. If only I could have scooped faster, or eaten less product, for sure I would still be there today. Which would have been impossible because I would be dead at thirty after drinking four-scoop milkshakes for lunch every day. Wisely, I would never work in a place that sold food again.

I worked at my next job for six years. Still with no solid plans on going to university, and zero plans on becoming a confident person, I showed up to my interview at the Cameleon Vert outdoor furniture store in Montreal wearing all the makeup I had bought from the Body Shop that was adjacent to Laura Secord, very high platform sandals I bought on my break one day while sipping a chocolate shake, and a skin-tight dress. I didn't really know what to wear to a job interview but wanted to look grown-up. I got the job because no one else had applied.

The Cameleon was housed in a nineteenth-century building on the edge of Old Montreal. The owner had created a true work of beauty—inside was a manufactured rain forest in the middle of one of Canada's coldest cities. He imported furniture and plants from warm climates, made cascading bouquets for well-heeled customers, and was one of the grumpiest people I have ever met, as though all the beauty he had to give was in the store. He was curt, at times hostile, and always right. Even though he was wrong a lot. To the owner's credit, though, he paid more, a lot more, than minimum wage. Occasionally, I will see what minimum wage is and think, *I was making that twenty years ago*. But I worked hard for it, unloading trucks filled with pottery and cast-iron furniture, lifting plants that weighed more than I did, and staying late to close a fancy store in a bad part of town. I loved a lot of that work: getting dirty, using my body, performing feats of strength, wearing overalls every day. It suited me. The average customer was wealthy, or hoping to be wealthy one day, and I learned a new language: How to Give Rich People What They Want but Not at a Discounted Price.

My first few weeks were really tiring, and at the end of a long day, I tripped over a vase and it broke. It cost $225, and I cried until I couldn't breathe. That was my rent, and I wasn't even living paycheque to paycheque yet.

My manager came by and kicked another vase, and it broke, too. He said, "Shit happens, Alicia." That was when I learned about how much retail goods are marked up. The answer is: a lot.

It was a dysfunctional place that always took me back after failed short-lived attempts to try new jobs. The store managers and staff all cared for me, which I needed, because I was lost, just a young woman living in the city for the first time, surviving on Lean Cuisines, Du Maurier Lights, and white wine from the corner store. This is how a lot of my retail jobs have been: interesting people who were, like me, unsure of how to get along in the "normal" world. At the time, I really was unhappy working at this beautiful store. I felt directionless, and instead of enjoying the freedom I had from nineteen to twenty-four, I was a bag of nerves. I would work long days and often walk home in the dark and cold to my little apartment on the edge of Westmount and Notre-Dame-de-Grâce and hang out with my friends who were all in school and try not to think about why I wasn't. I didn't understand anything, but at least I had people I could ask.

Really, working at the Cameleon was a great job. The responsibility meant that I eventually figured out I had to wake up and be on time and couldn't lie in bed all day if I wanted to pay rent and eat. It taught me to be accountable to my co-workers, and every day there was the small satisfaction of helping people: making their homes more beautiful, composing bouquets of flowers for lovers and lost ones. There is meaning and purpose in each day in a store.

Working in retail is a good place for people pleasers, people who like to make other people happy. People who like control and making their own rules and Back in Five Minutes signs that start the moment someone actually reads the sign.

When I started working in clothing stores, I thought this would be my ticket to cool, but it was more of a ticket to being broke but having beautiful clothes. I worked on Saint Laurent Boulevard during the late

1990s, and the store I worked in was open from ten a.m. to midnight, had a DJ, and was filled with the coolest staff and the worst customers. The owner was an angry young man, paranoid from pot and the fear of being caught for smuggling counterfeit jeans into foreign lands. He hired me because he thought I was Jewish, and even though I corrected him many times, he didn't believe me until he saw me eating a sausage sandwich, and then he unleashed his recent fervour for religion on me in the back room. There were dark days at that shop that were balanced out by so much laughter, so much dancing, and the fun that Saint Laurent was just before it became too upscale for stores like that. It was the first place I worked where the staff spent most of what they earned in the store, getting first dibs on the locally made designer jeans, Champion track pants, and beautiful but uncomfortable Red Wing boots or, worse, American Apparel T-shirts that would shrink in cold water. We all spent so much of our hard-earned money there and the rest of it at bars after work, kissing fun people and getting bladder infections from particularly handsome men. It was a short-lived and necessary time in my life to learn that maybe having cool clothes wasn't enough for a good life. But it was a close second in those days.

Soon thereafter I started more of a professional trajectory in retail, entirely by accident. I was living in Vancouver, quickly running out of money, and got the first job I applied for: assistant manager at a fancy-ish, designer-ish clothing store on Robson Street. I had to wear a suit (which was a great look with my shaved head) and appear professional, while making fart jokes to the other managers as soon as the store was empty. I remember thinking $25,000 a year seemed like a lot of money when they offered me the job but realizing when I got my first paycheque that it was barely enough to live on and buy the new clothes each season that we were expected to wear. There is some status in simply working at a store like that, I guess, because you get to help hapless wealthy people make short-sighted decisions to buy expensive clothing. The store had two floors, a marble staircase, security guards, locked cases of costume jewellery and beaded bags, and gowns that would often sell not to adults but to children for sweet sixteen parties and proms.

One of my favourite customers was the notorious and glamourous woman who owned the most upscale massage parlour in town. She would come in once a month with a new and beautiful young man on her arm and choose one of us to help her shop. It was very important not to look directly at her companion. Doing so might mean losing a $5,000 sale, and we worked on commission, so our eyes never wandered to the Adonis beside her. Well, almost never: if you weren't helping her, you could look all you liked, but from behind a mannequin. The worst customers were the organized crime shoplifters who would choose very busy times, or times when we were short-staffed, and then walk away with a rack of clothing. My favourite day working there was the eve of Y2K, New Year's Eve 2000, when the fear that failing computers might lead to outright anarchy was so strong that we stayed late to protect the store from looters and rioters. We locked up worried that the store we cared for might not be standing the next day. Of course it was, which, in many ways, was too bad.

The last clothing store I managed was a yoga shop on Granville Island, one of the busiest tourist destinations in Canada. I hadn't actually done yoga before, and still really loved smoking, but it was a "great opportunity" to spend five years asking what a person who wants to detox until a plug of mucus comes out of their butt wants to wear when they are done in the toilet (trick question: they are never done in the toilet). Anyway, the answer was always the Om T-shirt and the tie-dyed organic leggings. I probably sold 400 Om necklaces there. The trick was to put out a few Oms so the right om could find the right owner, chosen based on energy emitted by the factory-made om, one of dozens kept in a bag under the counter. A customer might be stretching or in Warrior pose the entire time I was helping them. It was a lovely store, with a meditation corner for testing out handmade cushions or taking a moment away from the intensity of Granville Island and the unceasing hum of its pan flutes. Occasionally, staff from other stores would come in to inhale our lavender-scented air, crack a self-help book, and just breathe. It was a special place, and the people who worked there were special to me. Smart and often lost for a moment in life.

My last retail job was the last. I was in my mid-thirties and found myself working as a nutritionist in a pharmacy. It wasn't a bad job, but I grew tired of seeing good people who were staring down cancer or MS wait patiently for help while a person with health and wealth expected zippier, more chipper service than I could provide. I broke that year. Tired of owners working us to exhaustion with no benefits. Tired of waking up and trying to be kind to people who would always look down on people in retail.

But there is so much I miss! I miss the little rewards: a clean store, a beloved customer (too many to name, too many to count). And I miss the friends. The big bonus in working retail is that when no one is in the store, you can really be yourself, and you build deep friendships with co-workers. You also create a language to communicate around the customer, perfecting meaningful looks to let someone know the person you are serving is a jerk. In every store I have worked in, I have made friends for life. Which is worth every bad day, bad customer, and bad boss I ever had.

I think back to the woman in the drugstore, still working retail in her sixties. Not only could I have been her, but I respect her. Next time, if I am unsure which cash register to use, I will just quietly go to self-checkout and give her a break.

WE DO NEED MATH

Some people say we don't need math after high school. Incorrect. Of course we need math every day to manage life. This being said, I passed high school math by only one point and risked not graduating because I was so bad at it. Sure, since then my mother has said that she assumes I had a learning disability and isn't sure why I wasn't helped, but that's okay, the arts were for me! However, I often think about what we could study in our youth to better set us up for a long life of learning how to pay back debt, how to grocery shop, how to have an argument without feeling like you might die afterward. And how about how to quietly toot when you really need to toot?

Most importantly, on a late-summer afternoon, I wished I had learned how to save wildlife, specifically, on this day, a pigeon. Mostly because I had already figured out that tooting thing. Basically, I have a master's degree in silent tooting.

My friend Jasmine and I were drinking coffee in the small outdoor area behind Paper Crane, a coffee shop nestled on the same block as the Korean grocer and the doctor of traditional Chinese medicine. Paper Crane is a *real* coffee shop. They have a small selection of pastries and a very good barista. The coffee is rich and chocolatey; it will make you fly for at least an hour. Jasmine and I meet there as it is equidistant from her place and mine, and as the September sun beat down on us in the parking-lot-cum-café, we heard something rustle. Sorry, I just wrote "cum café." What is wrong with me?

Anyhow, we heard something moving. Was it our stomachs reacting to the strong coffee? Would I need to silently toot? We listened again. The sound was coming from behind a bucket of cooking oil that was stored beneath an open staircase. It didn't sound like a good noise. It sounded like a hurt noise. I investigated and, in doing so, scared an injured pigeon into a crack between the staircase and cement wall. Now it was trapped. *Way to go, Tobin,* I thought. *You are a genuine idiot. Sure, you can fart imperceptibly, but now is not the time to gloat.* The terrified bird was trying to hide from me, but it was stuck. Its beautiful wings were pressed up against the sides of the crack, and underneath its small red feet was just a hole. This was not good. This pigeon deserved better.

I stepped away and tried to convince myself that this was the pigeon's Temple Grandin hug machine it just liked to spend time in when it was scared. Maybe all the more introverted local pigeons did this when they needed a time out from the group.

Jasmine and I drank coffee and periodically checked on the bird where it remained, flinching at our approach but otherwise unmoving. The SPCA would require us to catch the bird if we were to get it help. We both knew this because in Vancouver—despite the best efforts of wildlife to coexist with humans—I don't know many people who haven't had to call for help for a bird before. I got down on the ground and tried to see how I could safely remove the bird from its oily prison. The pavement was hot and dusty, and small bits of gravel dug into my shins and palms. The chances of breaking the pigeon's wings seemed so high, and whenever I took a gentle hold of its shaking body, it burrowed a bit deeper into the crack.

I followed Jasmine into Paper Crane to ask the barista if she knew anything about this pigeon. Perhaps my theory that the bird was very shy was true? No such luck. It had hit an electrical wire and fallen about an hour before and was hiding behind the oil bucket last time she saw it (a few minutes before I scared it into the crack). She had been checking on the bird during her rare moments of quiet, between making cappuccinos, Americanos, and flat whites. We explained the new situation and she provided us with gloves, a tea towel, salad tongs, and a large plastic spatula. The barista was now part of our very elite rescue group. I set to work, with Jasmine's direction, on Operation Pigeon Extraction. I wanted to help. If it wasn't for me, this poor animal might already be back up flying and pooping on everything.

I was shaking as I lay down on the dusty ground of the parking lot, and the ache of my frozen shoulder (a real condition, not something made up, like jelly hoof or ringworm) reminded me that *my* wings weren't doing so great either. I pulled the gloves on and gently put one hand underneath the bird. Its body was a wonderland. How could anything be as light and as soft and as hollow-feeling as a bird, and have such power and grace, that you can see if you have eyes in your head and a heart in your chest? The pigeon recoiled, understandably, as a human (I don't think birds wax poetic about our string-bean bodies and angry lives) touched it. The bird's wings made a desperate papery noise as they scraped against the cement walls. I let go. Sweat stung my eyes, and if I'd had to silently toot at this time, I couldn't.

I stood up and the parking lot was spinning. That coffee was really strong, the pigeon was so small, the sun was so hot, and my heart was beating so hard that I thought I might puke. Jasmine and I decided to try a new approach, with her taking the spatula in one hand to protect the bird's head and keep it from pushing forward as I tried to gently pull it backwards and out. It didn't work. We did this a few more times. Carefully, we made progress, taking a break every few minutes, and then starting again. My shoulder was screaming, and I was holding my breath. Finally, the pigeon was free.

For a moment. The dazed and terrified bird then flew directly into the café door and fell, got up again, flew into the café, and hit the front window. Hard.

Jasmine, the barista, and I cornered the pigeon, caught it in the tea towel, and managed to get it outside. This time, the bird hopped up onto a planter and rested.

By now, the café had closed, so Jasmine and I gathered our things and agreed this was a triumph of sorts and hoped the pigeon recovered in time for sundown.

I slowly walked home, and I felt good. I felt really good about who we were and what we did that day, and I wished that in school we were taught this as well: how to save small and delicate animals when they don't know they need us to. Maybe somewhere in all those math equations it says three women + one tea towel + a spatula + compassion = a free bird.

HOW TO TALK TO CITY ANIMALS

Each day I look forward to a time when I can pack up my life and move to a small town, buy a little place, and start my own artisanal bread-making business, or kombucha empire, or even better, wiring old pottery bits into $800 lamps. I will have a menagerie of farm animals, including a baby goat or two, a pony wearing a sweater, a cow that loves to hug, and some small pigs that will become huge pigs. The townsfolk will laugh at the City Kid who falls for an old country trick, like selling a little pig that is actually a big pig in disguise. But I will arm my pigs and run those people right out of town. I mean, I will laugh, too, sitting on top of my piles of lamp-making money while dipping my arbutus-wood goblet into the kombucha fountain I'll install in my minimalist farmhouse-inspired kitchen. Either way, we all win, with laughter.

Although those days are surely just around the corner, I know I don't have to move to the country and learn stuff that is hard—like making things and lifting things and being polite—when cool animals and beautiful trees are already all around me. Each day I try to take in (not literally, as that is theft; I have been warned) the natural beauty of the parks and gardens all over my city. When communing with nature, I find talking to local animals to be the most rewarding pursuit, and I encourage you to start there, because petting trees isn't that much fun! (Although it is, admittedly, *some* fun.) And remember this important rule: your neighbour's pets are also your pets if the pets are outside. If you actually get invited inside someone's house in the city? Run.

Now here are some other tips for yakking with city animals (tragically, rarely yaks):

1. Dogs: I am not here to argue the merits of dogs versus cats. For our purposes here, they are basically interchangeable.[1] A dog in the city is a free antidepressant. You won't even believe how good you feel after meeting one, or how bad your hand is about to smell. Say you are out and about and you see a dog. You are going to want to talk to that dog, and then, if things go well, you are going to ask the dog if he would like to be pet. You are probably thinking this is like dating, and I can honestly say, I have no idea. I do know about dogs, though. Just say hello to the dog, as simply as possible, in a very dumb voice: HALLO DAWG! If he wags his tail, it's a go. If he tucks his tail, or looks away, or lays his ears flat, it is a non-consensual pat. Do not touch the dog. Dogs do not speak the same language we do but can communicate big thoughts with simple gestures. If the owner of the dog doesn't stop, they (either species) obviously have IBS and must get home. You can still reach out your hand as the dog walks past you and get a touch of the soft fur, though not the owner's. Do not touch the owner. If the dog's owner tugs the dog away from you *even though the dog has indicated that a nice hello and hearty pat would be*

1 For the record, dogs are better, as they were bred to fill up the emptiness inside our hearts.

appreciated, you have run into what I call a Jerk Dog Owner, and they probably just had a hard day and don't want to interact with humans, or they just need to get home to use the toilet. Sure, it would be nice if they gave you one sweet moment with their pup, but would you if it meant you might shit yourself? I think not. Don't worry, though, all of this dog conversation will eventually become non-verbal, but that can take years, especially if you have never had a dog of your own. Remember, a dog is happiness tied to a human, so maybe say hello to the human, too. Based on my research, there is a ninety percent chance that if you follow my advice, you will get to talk to a dog today and a seventy percent chance you will get to pet one.

2. Cats: You are going to have to work a bit harder here, but it is worth it. Softer and more vain than dogs, cats are everywhere, and they almost never have a human tied to them. Not all cats are interested in making contact with humans, sometimes not even the humans who keep them alive. But chances are good that, every now and again, a cat will approach you and want to be pet, without needing much, or any, coaxing. The easiest scores are the fat ones, who have tiny legs and like to roll around on the sidewalk. Maybe they are trying to get up, I can't be sure, but get in there and pet that cat. Give the cat's ears a gentle scratch. If the cat likes it, they will invite more interaction. Do not start by petting the cat's belly, or as I like to call it, their snack shack. That is a danger zone. Even the fattest cat can turn into a bear trap in a split second, catching your well-meaning hand in sharp claws and jaws. Anyhow, if you see a lovely cat on a porch, and the cat makes eye contact with you, call out something very flattering to the cat; they love compliments. May I suggest something

like, YOU LOOK LIKE A SMALL LION AND YOU ARE CLEARLY SUCH A REGAL ANIMAL WOULD YOU CONSIDER LOWERING YOUR STANDARDS AND ALLOWING THIS LOWLY HUMAN A SCRITCH OF YOUR FINE EAR? If the cat wants to take it to the next level, they will let you know by coming for a visit, rubbing up against your legs, and generally cheering you up. If you see a cat in a window, just give them a wave; they like that, too. Cats are the softest and do not smell hardly at all, unless they ate something really bad or they are very old. And even then they don't smell nearly as bad as a dog does just generally.

3. Squirrels: One thing's for sure, if you know someone who calls squirrels rats with fancy tails, lose that person's number. Quick. If they don't see the beauty in everyday animals like the common squirrel, they shouldn't be invited to parties, if people are still having parties these days. Are they? I haven't been invited to one in years. Weird. The trick with squirrels is to not startle them, which is virtually impossible, at first. Of all the animals I like to observe, I rate squirrels pretty high, because they are very graceful and hardly ever seem to be eating garbage. Do not try to touch squirrels, but do say hello. I have noticed over time that they relax a bit and like to be told nice things about their almond-shaped eyes and quick bodies. Word to the wise: never let a squirrel inside your house. They will destroy it, and also piss everywhere.

4. Pigeons: I once saw a pigeon and he, like most pigeons, had a beautiful coat of feathers, dove grey tinged with peacock blues and greens, all made more striking by his beautiful orange beak. One of his feet had been crushed, and he was perfectly balanced on just one

foot, pecking at the pavement for bits of food. This small, peaceful, humble bird struck a chord deep within me. A place inside that understood being different and struggling just to survive. And I realized in that moment that pigeons get a really bad rap. And then he took flight and his little leg did not impede him in any way. He was breathtaking. When speaking to a pigeon, use soft tones and state the obvious. Pigeons are great but messy and dirty. If you must touch, wash hands 1,000 times.

5. Crows: Someone out there is going to love crows so much that they will write me and say something about how crows are superior in all ways, and so misunderstood, and I will write back and say, *I know, everyone knows that, uh-duh*, and that I am building a crow army based on my long-standing crow behaviour research, so they'd better sleep with one eye open, because that way they can meet the crow that takes their life. Crows are great animals but only towards other crows, and even then, all crows are like older, mean siblings that think it is fun to hurt you. So you have to be smart about creating a relationship with your neighbourhood crows. When crows are not nesting, they are safe to approach, and I recommend saying good morning, afternoon, or evening if you find one who is late to returning to the hell they surely must come from. Even more than cats, crows love to be told they are beautiful. I suspect that's because, much like us, they feel like deep down inside they are truly unlovable and need constant reminders that this is untrue. I believe that crows would take the most selfies if they had Instagram. Talking to crows is a great investment in your outdoor experience, as they will remember

you for your kindness, and within two or three years, you will be considered friend and not foe.

6. Raccoons: Probably best that you just circle the block or get a new place to live if one is on your lawn. Respect the raccoon. Give them their space. Do not talk to or feed. No exceptions. Wait, one exception. If you call out to one, from a distance, you're letting it know you're there and giving it a chance to get a head start if it has babies with it. You want to give an animal this potentially dangerous, essentially as dangerous as it is cute, an awareness that you are out and about. This probably won't make them move. If you do decide to speak to a raccoon, tell it it's extremely smart and that you respect it.
7. Skunks: Best-looking animal. Give it a lot of space. They have a lot of junk in the trunk and can't move so fast, but they are adorable, so you can laugh at nature's creation: a beautiful, gentle animal with a huge butt. You may talk to a skunk, but, like, from about a block away. I recommend letting a skunk know as soon as possible that you are about a block away. Make sure it doesn't panic and run right at you, which can happen with the young ones, and simply cross the street! Whisper that you love them. They will catch it on the wind.
8. Mice and Rats: Personally, I like screaming, so seeing a rat or a mouse is just another excuse to scream and scream! I do also enjoy how graceful they can be when running. Everyone has beauty. Mice and rats are very different, but if you see either in your house, give it a heads-up that the bad man is coming!

See how I commune with nature each day by taking walks to and from the liquor store or the farmers' market or my friend's house, who never seems to be home even though I see the curtains move a bit when I ring the doorbell? And if someone like me can commune with nature in the middle of a bustling city, you can too. Just follow my handy tips and remember: that pottery/lamp-building thing was my idea.

STANDING UP AND BEING FUNNY

When did I start doing comedy? At birth. When I was born, the doctor handed me the tiniest microphone. It was a lot of pressure, but I did a tight five minutes of clean material (which says a lot for a baby) and got one applause break before they handed me to my mother to nurse. So technically, I have always been a comedian. A comedian you have probably never heard of.

Comedy was important to my family. It was who we were. We liked to kid around. My parents loved comedy: albums, shows, and movies. My mother and father never censored our viewing in the world of comedy. We watched Cheech & Chong (which was strange because my parents are so straight and never smoked weed) and Monty Python, listened to Eddie Murphy (okay, you got me, Eddie Murphy's specials were censored, but his albums were okay to listen to), stayed up late every Saturday night to check in on the Coneheads, and did characters from *Second City Television* to make each other laugh. My father loved John Belushi and showed us *The Blues Brothers* in the theatre and then countless times on our VCR. My mother was a huge fan of Mel Brooks. We would watch *Young Frankenstein*, and any time we hugged our mother she did a beautiful Madeline Kahn impression, begging us not to touch her hair or nails. I mean, I *think* it was an impression! Our home was filled with terrible impressions of impressions: Gilda Radner's Baba Wawa, Dana Carvey's Church Lady, Mr. Bill, and the especially wonderful and hilarious Toonces the Cat.

But no one made me laugh the way Steve Martin did in *The Jerk*. Martin's character, Navin Johnson—an adopted child raised in a family he loved but couldn't always relate to, who loved tuna sandwiches and wasn't too smart—became the archetype for everything that was and would always be funny to me: gentle, naive, hopeful but hapless, and loving. Navin Johnson was blown away by the world. He trusted everybody and believed in the good in everyone. He loved his dog. He loved his lady. He loved his family. And he just wanted to be successful so they could be proud of him. I related to him so much as a kid and still do as an adult. *The Jerk* is my *Star Wars*. *The Jerk* is my *Breakfast Club*. *The Jerk* is my *Titanic*.

I loved to make people laugh. I would dance. Fall. Do a silly voice. I loved the attention. And it made me feel accepted, like I belonged, like I was good at something. Early on, I learned how to tell a joke and set up a prank, how to wait for the right time to break into a fake tap-dancing routine (always the right time, I promise). I was the class clown, if they would have me (it seemed to depend on the year when I was in elementary school, but by high school I was voted the funniest person each year except one, because that year I was working on being cool and failed).

The first time I was ever onstage in a comedic capacity was in grade five, so I was about twenty. The female students were fighting so much that the school intervened to try to rebuild friendships. They decided we should mount an all-female production of *You're a Good Man, Charlie*

Brown. Jenn, a lovely peacekeeper type, was to be Charlie Brown; shy Cheryl was Snoopy (one of the bigger roles, to help her come out of her shell); and I was going to be the Narrator (a behind-the-scenes role to help me calm the fuck down). Cheryl and I traded roles immediately. Finally, even more attention for me! I practised so hard. I remember stepping out that night thinking how great I was going to be, but when my feet touched the gymnasium stage, and I started speaking as Snoopy, time felt like it stopped and the room spun. I spoke too quickly, and I forgot some lines and remembered others. I was ashamed for trading with Cheryl (and a bit regretful, too; that narrator role was pretty sweet).

In the end, I learned I wasn't going to be the star of every show. But the play also helped. I had transferred to that school at the end of the previous school year, and it was a bumpy transition to say the least. I didn't have any female friends in my class that year. I was acting out a lot, my grades were poor for the first time in my life, and I felt alone. It was also that awkward stage where how you look and dress start to create status among children, and I had no style and certainly no status.

Home wasn't much better. During the summer, our house had flooded while we were away on a rare vacation, and we were living in a construction zone, both parents working day and night to repair the roof over our heads and keep us fed and clothed. That little play helped me make real friends, ones that I still have to this day.

In high school, I lived in a place in Quebec that still had anglophone schools—schools with dwindling numbers, to be sure, and dwindling budgets most definitely. Most of the school budget went to the music program, but I couldn't learn to read music; like math, it would make my cheeks hot and my stomach twist, so I sought out everything that wasn't music or math. I took any drama or visual arts class I could, learning to work a camera, the satisfaction of developing my own film outweighing the smell of developing my own film. I learned to paint and draw and sculpt, I took shop, I excelled at baking and failed miserably at sewing. Our art teacher ran drama classes at lunch and a small group of us would run lines, make skits, be overly dramatic. The older grades would put on a yearly variety show with kids doing their best versions of characters they created or ones from TV. I dreamt of being asked to be in it, but it was all guys. Girls were only props. I didn't want to be a prop. So I waited.

As a young person I was outspoken, idealistic, with zero real-world experience to draw from, and hilarious—sometimes. I was emotional, prone to depression, and spent days hiding at home from the pressure of school, friendships, and late assignments. I was one of those children who live in a room so messy you can't be sure they're actually in the room. Everything was overwhelming. I was deeply insecure about how I looked, how I dressed, if I was liked, and this anxiety didn't make for the easiest teenage years. I was also the kind of kid who bullied bullies, which was weird. I would get into real fights at the drop of a pin. With the little I had, I was a lot.

My sense of humour smoothed over a ton and helped me make and keep a few friends. I was still devoted to *Saturday Night Live*, but in 1989, when I was fourteen, the CBC introduced *The Kids in the Hall*, probably one of the best sketch shows that will ever be. It was informed, it was silly, and it had Buddy Cole, ex-male model and self-proclaimed "faggot." Scott Thompson was a gorgeous man who had as much courage as he had laughs, and he was the brightest star. Being a kid in a small town and feeling different and not knowing a lot of the real world and seeing some of it through the eyes of these comedians, these Canadian comedians who still looked like kids themselves (except Kevin McDonald: he always looked like he was old enough at least to buy beer) meant that maybe there was room in the world for the way I thought and the way I wanted to live. Humour was changing, and I was excited. Bye, bye Church Lady, and hello Chicken Lady! My friends and I would rehash the best of that week's episode, proud that this Canadian show was so funny, and even recognized as funny *by Americans*. I still have a tendency to explain the My Pen sketch at least once a year to a millennial desperate to get away from me. See, it's his special pen, and if someone touches his pen ... Hey, where are you going, young lady?

In my last years of high school I got involved in the annual variety show, and in grade ten (we only go to grade eleven in Quebec, because that's when the budget runs out and you are pushed into the real world of poutine farms) I signed up for the Macho Man contest that happened during the Winter Carnival. I think the origins of the Macho Man contest were innocent—some teenage boys wanted to make the school look at their muscles or something—but by the time it reached us, it was the funny boys against the good-looking guys, trying to get the school to admire their muscles. This just in: I had muscles, too. So I signed up and created a character called Velveeta the Cheesy Lady, based loosely on a character from *The Jerk* called Patty Bernstein, a sexy carnival daredevil who takes Navin Johnson's, ugh, innocence in so many ways. I was the first girl to ever sign up for the contest, and I won. It was probably a combination of flexing my muscles and dancing in a skimpy bathing suit while throwing slices of cheese. But it established my dominance as a funny person, a feminist, and a pretty sexy dancer—things that are still true today.

When high school was over, so was the chance to be onstage without much training. I applied for theatre school but chickened out when I was called back for a second audition, my mother screaming in the background that actors are losers, which is often but not always true. I was aimless. I dropped out of college and moved into the city. I made my friends and people at work laugh. I started going to comedy clubs, secretly wishing I could be onstage and loudly making suggestions to the improv troupes. My friend Mike Paterson was becoming an actual stand-up comedian, but I couldn't figure out how to ask him how to do it. I wanted to be seen and heard but had no clue how. Part of the problem was that I didn't see women doing comedy. I did on TV, but in real life, it was ninety-nine percent men. I didn't see anyone like me, so I didn't think comedy was for me. People would tell me I should be a comedian, and I believed them, but doing it was an entirely different thing.

When I was twenty-six, I signed up for an improv class. I showed up thinking it was a comedy improv class, but it was filled with actors wanting to learn to, I don't know, pretend they were human? Good luck, actors! The teacher was a comedian and I think we were both bummed out at the lack of humour in these actors. My boyfriend encouraged me to keep with it, but I think that was because he was having an affair on improv night. Pretty good joke on me!

About two years later, at the end of a political science class that I was taking in Vancouver, my professor approached me and said that the continuing education program was offering a stand-up writing class and she deeply felt I should give it a try. No one that smart had ever told me

I should be a comedian, and I wanted her approval so bad, so I signed up. The caveat of the class was that, no matter what, at the end of the six sessions, you had to get onstage and do five minutes of jokes you had written. The first class was filled with an ex–football player, a real estate agent, a nurse, someone obsessed with cats, and a very young man named Ivan Decker, who I think was eighteen at the time. None of us except the eighteen-year-old had ever written a joke before. The class was fun, and the teacher made writing jokes easy; it was a formula and every punchline had to be about "crackheads." I never wrote a crackhead joke, which—let's face it—is a bit of a badge of honour, but I did write five minutes of pretty rude comedy à la early Sarah Silverman, including blow job jokes and incest jokes. I won't lie, it wasn't that bad (for a first-timer; if I were still doing that set now, it would be truly horrible). It turned out I could write a joke, and I could tell a joke, and I could help other people write a joke. I was good at punchlines. I'd had a lot of practice making people laugh, and it paid off. But I had no practice being onstage at all. The last time was when I sang Bachman-Turner Overdrive's "Takin' Care of Business" with my friend Mike at a CEGEP college event while pretty stoned.

As the night neared, my friends bought tickets and the pressure was on. I knew I couldn't back out. Even my therapist showed up. I can remember looking at Ivan and thinking he would be famous one day and telling him as much. We each got up and took turns doing our first five minutes and I don't remember any of it; it was like I was Snoopy all over again. Someone approached me after I got offstage in this small, strange Greek restaurant on Commercial Drive and told me I was ready for TV and handed me her card. It turned out that person wasn't a great judge of talent, but I would find that out later when I did one of her all-female comedy competitions and lost.

I thought I would be a person who did stand-up comedy, but I didn't know what to do next. When the class ended, I finished school and moved home to Montreal for a year. With the exception of one show, at every open mic I did in Montreal I bombed. Hard. No matter what I did, I bombed. I bombed sober, I bombed drunk, I bombed. I bombed in front of some really great Canadian comedians that year, and when I meet them now, they don't remember me, because what I didn't know back then was that bombing is normal and rarely memorable. My desire for perfection, which held me back so much in life, held me back tightly in comedy, and it would be another two years before I tried again, back in Vancouver.

It was 2007. I don't remember how I figured out how to get on the amateur night at Yuk Yuk's. I think it was really simple: I emailed and a comedian named Pete Johansson gave me a spot. He approached me after my set, when I was reeling from nerves. I had just done all my dumb jokes for over 100 people, in a real comedy club, and they seemed to like them. He said something like, "You're funny. There aren't a lot of women working right now. If you email me, you can have a spot every second week."

I knew a good offer when I heard it and accepted. For at least a year, Pete was good to his word and put me on shows, and I got better. And every show, there was Ivan, my friend from class, destroying. I met comedians I am still friends with, like Charlie Demers, Graham Clark, Dave Shumka, Erica Sigurdson, Katie-Ellen Humphries, and I also met hundreds of people I will never see again. I *also* met people I wish I had never met. People who truly are the worst, but that is a list I keep in a different book (a book of prayers; I pray for them).

It was a huge opportunity to get stage time. I set a goal to do 100 shows in my first year. That was just two a week, but that was a lot in the already busy life of a woman in her early thirties with a full-time job, who was extremely attractive and almost never farted! I was old compared to the other people at the open mics and the amateur *Crash and Burn* show every week at Yuk Yuk's. There were advantages to being a bit older: I had social skills and a work ethic, and some life to draw from. But I lacked the energy and the blind confidence of some of the younger people, which could be a blessing or a curse. Stand-up attracts all sorts of weirdos—from the sweetest introvert to the most dangerous sociopath—and you all have to huddle backstage waiting your turn. It was also a time when Rohypnol jokes and other rape jokes seemed to be "edgy," and women, LGBTQ folks, and Muslims bore the brunt of a lot of jokes. It was uncomfortable, and it hurt to see people laugh at these lazy, terrible jokes. Why couldn't they laugh at themselves, or rich people? And sometimes a comedy show would have twelve men but just one woman per night. The atmosphere backstage was hostile, and it smelled like guys who didn't know how to shower or eat. But I waited my turn, and when I got onstage, I put all the energy I had built up sitting back there, buffering myself against the misogyny and racism onstage and off, into my set and got bigger and better laughs. Laughs I earned. I would walk back through the curtains and feel good about what I had said and who I was. At work the next day I would forget about being onstage the night before and go back to real life, selling yoga pants to people on juice cleanses. My friends started to introduce me as a comedian, but I didn't feel right saying it yet. After 100 shows, maybe.

Someone told me I had to try to get on to Graham Clark's show, *The Laugh Gallery*, which happened every Wednesday night on Commercial Drive. The only way to do that was to go down there and ask him for a spot. I hadn't met Graham yet, but I knew he was one of the best comedians in Canada already, and he was only twenty-six. I tried to get his attention after the show to ask for a spot, but he wouldn't make eye contact with me. He seemed shy and focused, but afterward, I realized he was tired of people asking him for stuff. Finally, with a few comedians around me, which made it even harder, I asked for a spot. He said something dismissive like, "Send me an email and I will get you on," when Jane Stanton spoke up and said, "She's funny. Give her a spot." And he did. And that is when I found my people.

I showed up the next week and did my set, watching Graham out of the corner of my eye, and he wasn't watching me, but he was listening, and he was laughing. To this day, few things feel as good as making that guy laugh. Everyone Graham booked was guaranteed to be funny, except the weekly wild card, an untested amateur or an out-of-town guest, and that week, and I think for that time only, I was the wild card. I loved walking from my little apartment in Strathcona, up Clark Drive, to the packed restaurant to watch or perform at *The Laugh Gallery*. It wasn't like Yuk Yuk's, where it felt like a bad set could be your last. People took risks, tried new jokes, and were themselves. The other comedians accepted me. When you wait your whole life for acceptance, and it is by a group of beautiful, kind, and talented weirdos, it is pretty overwhelming. Makes a person like me like herself. Helps her remember she is worth something.

It felt so great in those early days to fight through a set and win over a crowd. To get asked to perform on good shows that didn't pay or terrible shows that did pay. My peers always treated me like equals. But when I was asked to audition for the Just for Laughs Comedy Festival and wasn't chosen, and I started to see the political side more. And I started to see the sexism more. Pete left Yuk Yuk's and was replaced by someone who knew nothing about comedy, and then he was replaced by someone who knew even less. Men who weren't as funny as other (female) comedians were offered the best spots, the spots that let a comedian grow. I waited. I asked. But I was put on the back burner in favour of rape jokes, guys who drank with the manager, and a long white wave of men who could spend their lives kissing ass. I remember asking my friend Dave backstage if he wanted to be a professional comedian, Dave being one of the best comedians I have seen, and he laughed and said, "And hang out with these losers my whole life? No way." I kept having great sets but less and less at Yuk Yuk's and more and more at new shows, alternative shows, further and further away from the path I was told would get me to working full time as a comedian. Which I wasn't even sure I wanted anymore. Dave was right. What was I trying to do here?

In 2009, a bunch of us were being recorded as part of the NorthWest Comedy Festival for SiriusXM Satellite Radio. It was my first break, where people outside of Vancouver might listen to me lament about how beautiful sharks are and how an earthquake might not be the worst thing to happen to Vancouver because it might be the only thing that could liberate us from Lululemon. I was excited and nervous. Maria Bamford was there. MARIA BAMFORD. She was in a corner, quiet. All the local comedians piled into the small green room to check out the free drinks and food. Everyone was delighted because there was a huge charcuterie tray, and we ate cheese and deli meats and felt like stars, until a festival volunteer rushed in and took our meats away—explaining that the tray was for the American comedians—and replaced it with carrot sticks and ranch dip. That basically sums up what it is like to be a Canadian comedian at a Canadian comedy festival—we aren't even worth deli meat to the organizers, but those Americans can have all the rolled-up ham they like.

There were twelve comedians recording sets, and two women (Jane Stanton and I) were slotted in the first half. Best to get all the period jokes out of the way, am I right? I was ready. I had practised, I loved what I was wearing, and I felt so proud to be on this show. Then the host introduced me by saying: "Here is Alicia Tobin. She has huge tits." And that was the beginning of the end of my dream of being a stand-up comedian. It wasn't the first time something like that had happened. It was something gross, older male comedians would pull all the time. But this time I couldn't fight back. This was my opportunity, and this has-been, washed-up, middle-aged comedian had to take a bite. I thought about my father hearing that and fought back angry tears.

I did my set. I crushed. I got offstage and Maria Bamford said quietly to me that I had a good set.

Jane got up and he did the same thing to her. I felt faint, I pounded vodka sodas and got in a fight with my boyfriend, who was also a comedian. He said, "I told you it was like this. It isn't nice," and I walked home alone crying. He was right. He wanted to protect me from this. He didn't hold me back, and it was painful for him to see me going through this. He went through things, too, because we could only change comedy incrementally with our good jokes and kindness and safe and inclusive rooms. It was an uphill battle against the people who wanted to keep the status quo. It was the end of something I had half loved, and it forced me to create a different way of doing comedy. I was done with conventional stand-up; I just didn't know it yet.

For another year or two I kept at it. I did more and more alternative rooms. I started writing jokes almost exclusively about animals and shed the persona I hid behind that acted like she understood the world. I opened up my heart to the audience and showed them that I really didn't get life or the world at all! I was connecting with the audience, sometimes just a few people who seemed to like animals too. I could also eviscerate a heckler and then bounce back to the beauty of a raccoon.

But I was getting tired of men in comedy not treating women equally, not paying us to do shows, and not booking us for tours or comedy clubs. I was tired of trying to prove myself to people who weren't actually funny. Like, sure—a funnier person? Go ahead and oppress me. Fine. But these dullards? No way.

When I started drawing onstage, it was out of this anger. I was tired of my name being used to promote shows and getting nothing really in return. My group of friends I often performed with had gone in different directions, and it wasn't as fun to go to shows. I was angry at myself that I had given up on stand-up at clubs, and equally as angry at all the people who got in my way.

On the way to a show I really didn't want to do I bought markers and paper and had the idea that maybe the audience would like to draw something with me. That was it. I handed out paper and markers and asked the audience to draw something, and we looked at the drawings, and we laughed hard. This is where my show *Alicia Tobin's Come Draw with Me* came from, and this was how I was able to hang on to who I am, my beliefs about the world, the hope I have for people and who I want to be as a comedian. The show was based on the simple misconception that we should stop doing something we loved to do when we were kids because someone told us we weren't good at it. You don't have to be good at something to enjoy doing it—just think of all those comedians telling rape jokes!

Instead, I wanted to talk about animals and get to know strangers, and I wanted people to leave my show feeling good about themselves, so when my friend Chris Bentzen asked me if I wanted to do the show at his art gallery, I accepted. Chris and I thought the show would happen once or twice, but we ran it for three years. It sold out each month. We made something really special, where people could meet each other, draw, laugh, see amazing comedians who wouldn't attack them or drag them down into their pit of stink. And I could be me. I could be warm. I could show just how tough I wasn't. And how I really didn't get it (life, people, anything really), but the way I don't get is pretty much the same way none of us gets it. But that is no excuse to be unkind. It is no excuse to be angry. It is an excuse to open our lives to each other. Chris's art gallery also created a space for other similar comedians to figure some stuff out. It was hard to see it close in 2016. The last *Come Draw with Me* was emotional. My friends Charlie, Ivan, Ryan, and Kevin sang me out. I didn't know the show had meant something to them, too. It is just like me to not think I was doing anything good ever. Chris and I took a year off from doing the show, but we started it again in 2018, so ... come draw with me sometime?

Comedy was only as bad to me as it was good to me. And now that I've left the bad stuff behind, it has been so good to me. I think of that little kid watching *The Jerk*, laughing at how ambitious but lost Navin Johnson was, and know that we are the same. We just want to be loved, over anything else, and accepted for who we are: very dumb people who want deli meats.

SO YOU'RE A LITTLE SAD, SO WHAT? NICE THINGS TO SAY TO YOURSELF ON BAD DAYS

For Phillip Ontakos

You probably have no choice but to work today. You don't have the kind of job you can just not show up to and expect to have a job tomorrow. You need this job. And at work at least you can hate someone other than yourself for a moment: a rude customer, a co-worker who is a real ding-dong, or the other one who chews so loudly. Perhaps on the way home you find the energy to go to the grocery store, but once you get there, you suddenly have no idea how to make a meal. You leave with Windex and a jar of salsa. Mission accomplished! You get home and lie down. In the dark. Lying down is the best feeling. Has it been weeks like this? Crying. Cancelling on friends. Not returning messages. Does it feel like your brain is melting? Have you thought most days about ways to die and could not come up with a way that wouldn't hurt so many people? You don't remember a day where you felt hopeful. You go to work. You laugh when people laugh so they don't know that you can't really listen and nothing is funny right now. You go home. Eat something from a box. Shower. Sleep. Start again the next day. You don't know how to get through it outside of trying to follow some sort of routine.

Work. Sleep. Cry. Work. Sleep. Feel nothing.

I know this feeling, too. I have stopped wearing mascara so I could cry in the bathroom at work, staring up at the ceiling, hoping the tears would be reabsorbed before I had to go back out and answer the phone and ring through sales and be polite and mimic being engaged. It wasn't just that I was down, it was that everything had been going wrong for so long that the wheels had come off and I didn't know where to get new wheels. Listen, I don't drive, but you get the picture.

But then one day I stepped outside, and the sun was sort-of-well-kinda out. A sort-of-well-kinda-out sun on the West Coast is reason to celebrate. It was probably out before. I don't know. Small birds, the colour of the winter leaves, sprang from a shrub and I cried. I marvelled at how small those birds were and how perfect the day was. I was there. I was there to feel this day. In all that it was already and all of the who knows what it will be. Those birds were there with me (not for the whole day: no-birds-at-work policy). They had life to show me. I thought about how difficult it must be to be a bird and how scared they must feel when they are simply trying to eat. My heart burst for those birds because they were so exquisite. I began worrying I might become a weird bird person. Bird people are, like, sometimes, a lot. I laughed. I pushed forward. I saw so much. Stuff I walked past before. Houses returning to the earth in a slow defeat against the West Coast weather. Everything felt *more*. I felt like the world was showing off for me, but I may just have been waking up from being depressed for so long. Something broke through that day, and when my heart opened up, I quickly wedged something in to keep it from closing again.

And I then said to myself, "So you're a little sad, so what?"

I had been sad for a long time, pushing and pulling myself through life for about twelve months. But so what? I could still see beauty each day. All of this beauty kept seeping into my hardest and saddest places. It was lush green moss. It was kind words. It was a squirrel. And it was the lace around the shittiest of days. Like a fancy thong on a sunburnt butt.

I am so sad. But I see so much beauty. I see it in you. So if you woke up sad today, I am right there with you. I don't know what to do. I don't know how to fix it. Because I don't think it can be fixed. The world, people, well, they can be absolute dirty diaper garbage.

But you aren't. Say that to yourself for me:

"I am not dirty diaper garbage."

How did that feel? Better right? Now try this one:

"I will let the beauty of this world find me on my worst days."

And one other thing:

"I will believe the kind things people say about me and learn to know they are true."

And one more:

"Alicia, here is my credit card. Please go buy yourself a tiny horse."

I know, it is hard to feel that second-to-last one. Some days it feels like there is nothing left, like the cruel fist of the universe, or capitalism, has twisted the last bit of hope out of you. I know what that is like. That combination of fear of letting people down, of losing your job, of not being there. If you have to be there, carry something small in your pocket that reminds you of who you are. For years, I carried a piece of black onyx. It was small and smooth, and I could reach into my pocket and touch it. It was cool. And calm. Maybe someone out there is thinking, *Oh God, she's into crystals*, but I can assure you I am not. I mean, except crystals can totally heal cancer, if you find just the right crystal. Oh, did you choose the wrong one? But I loved that stone. Someone who knew me well gave it to me, and she believed in crystals, and I always made fun of her but also admired her, for her sense of wonder and her belief in magic. I can't say for sure that there is no magic. But I can for sure laugh at the idea of the healing power of crystals.

The part of me that hurts the most is the part that doesn't know I am any good. Or worth very much. That is the part that hurts the most when I hurt. The other part that hurts is my stomach because when I am upset, I eat so many cookies, you have no idea. But the first part, that part is the deep part. That part is being told I was ugly as a child. The part that always failed math. That part wasn't good at making friends. The part that made a toilet out of a basket and a plastic bag because I thought there was a vampire in the toilet at my house and was caught peeing in the basket with the plastic bag by my mother after she specifically asked me if I was making a toilet to pee into and I lied. And then I had to go use the vampire toilet to get rid of the pee. I have never been good at planning.

That hurt part is sticky, like a lint roller, and it seemed to pick up steam as I grew (you didn't have steam-powered lint rollers where you grew up? Too bad!). I took everything everyone ever said to me, out of their own hurt part, as the truth, and it hung on to me. By the time I made it to my twenties, I was mostly lint! I only believed the bad things people had said to me and internalized the difficult things that happen in life: friendships ending, heartbreak, bad employers, they were somehow all my fault and evidence of my unworthiness for happiness.

But living isn't just happiness, and if you count experience and heartache as measures of living, then technically speaking, I was living it up!

For that day when the world seemed to shake me out of my sadness for a moment and remind me it was still there, I am grateful. So, in my sadness, and on bad days, I know that outside of me is beauty. And inside, too. Even if today I can't see it.

What I am asking you is to remember:

You are good.

You are loved.

You are here.

And yes, you are sad. And the world is mostly awful some days. But there is magic here. There is wonder here. Your depression can be here, too. There is so much more here, more than the idea you had of yourself. Or the idea that mental health is not a real health issue. Here, there is no pressure to fix the breakup you can't mend, the past you can never get back. But you can make a difference by showing up as who you really are: a person who belongs here with all the other sad people with good hearts, who can see the moss on trees, who can hear the birds, and who can smell change in the air. You can be sad and happy at once. But you can't be one or the other all the time. Whichever you are today, you are the stars, you are the moon, and you are brilliant.

I don't know if this will help, but I made a little list of nice things you think about on bad days, and alphabetized them for easy reference:

A—Is for adultery: Someone you love cheated on you? That's bonkers. You are cool, smart, and kind. Don't let this destroy you. When you are ready, you need to let go of this person. They aren't the right person for you. A person cheats for a variety of reasons, and even if what motivated them was an issue in your relationship, you can't blame yourself. Take care of you right now. You are the only one who can.

Did you cheat on someone? Please go talk to someone. We all make mistakes. Be kind to yourself right now and face what is haunting you.

If your relationship is done, let go.

A—Animals! How cool are they? Please go to the internet and look at a baby aardvark right now! LOOK AT THEIR HANDS!

B—Butthurt: Okay, you took something way too personally because maybe, you know, you're just having a hard time. Nothing in life is fair. Look around at what you have and go out for a very cold drink. I highly recommend a lime Slush Puppie. Something better is coming your way, maybe even another, even slushier drink.

B—BUTTS! Everyone has one, and they're all cute!

C—Cunts! What? Say it! Hahaha, OH MY GOSH YOU CAN'T SAY THAT.

C—Cats! They are like house tigers! Check them out! Their eyes are like beautiful marbles!

C—Honourable mention: CAKE!

D—Dirty Dips (Donald Trump, for example). These people are seemingly everywhere; there are really only a few, but they are so awful that their stink spreads all over the place. Some people believe in hell just so they can hope these type of people get what they deserve one day. They probably won't, so definitely work to neutralize their effect on the world. You can counteract their wretched existence by upping your kindness game and using your gifts to make this world a better place.

D—Dogs. House wolves. As good as cats. It isn't a competition.

D—Honourable mention: DONUTS!

E—Envy. I know this well. It is hardest when you envy the life or success of a friend. You have to remember you are worthy of similar success, but this is their time. Unless they are a jerk. In which case, you can just let it all go.

E—Elegance. When you can walk from a buffet with three meals on one plate and look like you have your life put together. Now that is elegance!

F—Fuckheads! Say it! You CAN say it. Fuckheads are jerk faces x ten! They try to get you to do their work for them so they can go brown-nose with the boss. They check their text messages while running. They walk their dogs off leash. They tip ten percent on great service. They need a wake-up call but probably will just fall through an open manhole cover, be minorly injured and majorly compensated by a lawsuit, and drive around in their speedboat the one motherfucking day you get to go to the beach this year. FUCKHEADS!

F—Friends. This is it. They are everything. Thank them for loving you. Try to be a good friend. They are there for us when no one else seems to be. Hang on tight to the good ones and get rid of the bad ones.

G—Goop: Terrible website. Don't bother!

G—Good people. They are everywhere and waiting for an opportunity to do something good—maybe even great. You are one of them, and this lets you see that in other people. Don't give up hope. Don't fall prey to the idea that the world is mostly filled with bad people. You know it's not true, buddy.

H—Hellscape, i.e.: the world right now.

H—Hugs! They are great, as long as they are wanted.

I—Inappropriate comments: Call 'em out whether they are about you or someone else. Call out those racists, those 'phobes! We all belong here, and we are all in this together. No one is free until we are all free!

I—Ice cream. What the fuck? So good. Even the vegan kinds.

J—Jerks.

J—Joy.

K—Kleptocracy. See Dirty Dips.

K—Koala bear. Have you looked at one today?

L—Losers. Losers are people who have lost in life. Losers are people who take and take and give nothing back. Losers can be totally the worst!

L—Love, I guess. Give it. Wherever you can. Even when it hurts. Hold love in your heart and peace in your hands.

M—Misogyny: Ugh, this old chestnut. It is so awful and still so accepted. Kick it in the chestnuts!

M—Money. I love money.

N—Neglect. I think this is the saddest thing we can do to each other. I also think that neglect often demonstrates someone's inability to care for another or themselves. So much trauma.

N—Neapolitan ice cream! Underrated. See Ice cream.

O—Oligarchy! BARFIGARCHY!

O—Donuts are this shape.

P—Prisons: They don't have the right people in them a lot of the time.

P—Pie. It is as good as cake, if not better.

Q—Quakes. As in earthquakes? Hey, cut it out, Earth.

Q—Quiche! So good! You can put anything in there and it fancy! Highly recommend pepperoni sticks arranged in a heart or penis shape.

R—"Roxanne" by the Police. Please make it stop.

R—A robin redbreast signalling the much-awaited return of spring.

S—Slut shaming! Not good.

S—Sexy times! Really good!

T—TURD HATS! See Dirty Dips. A turd hat is a shithead but even worse because they are wearing a hat of poop.

T—Toffee. Any kind, even licorice, if that is all there is. Oh, and turtles and tortoises. They're totally tight!

U—Unwanted. This feeling hurts so much. You are wanted.

U—Umbrellas! What an invention. Round of applause for umbrellas!

V—Vampires! Not real.

V—Velvet: How sensual!

W—*Waterworld.* Yes, that movie that came out so long ago. Still not good!

W—Walruses: The elephants of the sea!

X—Xenophobia. The fear of someone different from you doing a better job than you, because you aren't good at stuff and you are a dangerous idiot.

X—Xenarthra: The order of mammals that sloths, anteaters, and the glorious armadillo belong to. Holy shit, eh?

Y—Yummy/yucky: Please don't say if you are an adult!

Y—You. Are. Wonderful.

Z—Zombie. I don't think all this zombie fan culture is healthy. What if that awful self-help book *The Secret* is real and all these zombie fans create a zombie apocalypse? No.

Z—Zebra. The zebra probably started out plain brown but kept evolving and adapting to stress and turned into a beautiful animal. Now that is amazing.

HASHIMOTO'S POTATO

2010

One morning I couldn't tie my own shoes. To be fair, I couldn't have tied anyone's shoes that day. My hips wouldn't bend, my hamstrings just stiff rods, my feet a million miles away. I was going to be late for work. So, there I was, in my early thirties, needing help tying my shoes. Already? Pain and insomnia were followed by the inability to fully wake up. Depression was a muddy blur and made me feel like there was a foot on my chest each morning. Well, I could live with that. I am extremely good at dragging my wagon. But I couldn't tie my shoes, and that was really a problem. Not that the other symptoms were not. I had no energy. My get-up-and-go had dwindled to gone. Exhausted, I was cancelling stand-up shows and avoiding my friends. My memory wasn't great, and I was forgetting people's names, even the names of people I knew well.

Back to my shoe-tying problem. Not ready for Ugg boots (over my dead body, and those of a few nude sheep), I went to see my doctor. I told her my symptoms, and she asked if I'd had my thyroid tested. I had not. What is a thyroid? It must be a pretty big deal if it can turn me into a sad marionette. My results from my thyroid-stimulating hormone blood test came back and I was hypothyroid, or low thyroid. I had many of the symptoms, some severe, but they were also the symptoms of many other conditions. I feel very lucky that my doctor tested my thyroid because the potential to be misdiagnosed, especially with depression, is high. She sent me home with a prescription for a thyroid replacement.

I had no idea what any of this meant, but I felt like I had an answer for the past many months of feeling completely off. I took the medication. Everything was going to be great! I gently patted myself on my back. And then, a few weeks later, my hair started to fall out. In clumps. Excellent! I could make a sweater to keep me warm.

It took a while for me to talk about this, as I was afraid that people would find out that I couldn't do, and didn't even want to do, things I once did, at least not all the time. I was concerned they'd see my insides, which are mostly soft, with some angry bits and maybe made of red thread. Keep in mind that until 2010, I didn't even know what a thyroid was, and I am still not clear what is going on in there exactly. Until recently, I thought babies came from belly buttons. And I was right. Don't let someone touch your belly button unless you can imagine them being the parent of your child one day.

The best part of the song "Hearts and Bones" by Paul Simon is when his lover asks why she can't be loved for who and where she is. Everyone is allowed to cry when it plays. But I had love in my life, no matter what was happening to my hair, or how altered I felt. I had kindness. I had family and friends. This is health in its own way. I knew it. I know it. Despite tremendous change and loss, I had and have a lot.

Should I apply those thoughts on love to my own body? Well, I guess I never thought about that kind of love. I do now. I don't worry as much about how I look in my bathing suit, or my jeans, or my bathing suit over my jeans, which looks pretty cool. This new skill of accepting myself shows up more and more. It is just a body, my body, doing its best, no better than any other, as genetics and environment roll through it. Just the one I have. The vessel, where I store my snacks and where my heart is. Even when my shoes seem so far away, or I magically put on ten pounds in a week, I am fine. Sometimes, I understand more, not about biology, but about other important things.

So, where was I? Hair loss. Okay, imagine the most beautiful hair in the world—like Scar from *The Lion King* but nicer, sexier. My mother use to call my hair my crowning glory, so you can imagine the amount of ego I had wrapped up in this hairdo, which was now all over the bed, the kitchen, my computer, my meals. My boyfriend would sweetly try to sweep it up before I noticed.

This was a side effect of the first pill I tried, a very mild dose, nothing to worry about, according to my doctor. She wasn't aware it was a side effect of that medication until I told her. She recommended that I buy a better-quality shampoo, perhaps "a Pantene." I remember thinking that I buy much fancier shampoo than my doctor. One of us had to get our priorities straight (her). Also, I began to worry that maybe this magic pill that works for millions of other people wasn't working for me. My heart began to beat really fast, and the room seemed to get smaller. Turns out, that was the medication, too.

Typically, one is given thyroid hormone replacement drugs for low thyroid. My desired treatment—wearing mittens and sleeping all day—wasn't available by prescription. Perhaps one day in the future, health care will catch up to the specific needs of the individual patient instead of thinking all of us want to return to the vibrant person we once were.

The idea of being on medication for the rest of my life scared me. I am drawn to a healthy lifestyle, I eat a healthy diet, unless you have chips, and then I eat chips. Your chips. I take them, and I eat them. Or a Dairy Queen Peanut Buster Parfait—those are like medication for the soul. Until they hit your stomach, and then they are like diarrhea for your butt.

Since this first pill was causing all of these side effects (hair loss, heart palpitations, anxiety), I decided to go the natural route and, with the supervision of my doctor, go off my medication. At this point, I thought my thyroid was just lazy and the right supplements or food might fix it. I mean, that is what Google told me. Google always right! Google all knowing.

2011

I went to see a natural healing practitioner—I thought he was a naturopathic doctor, but I looked at his website today and he is a "health detective." Well, that sounds official. In hindsight, I should have done a little bit, just a tiny wee tiny little tiny smidge, more research into this "practitioner." I also wish I knew at the time that some of the treatments he gave me, especially Lugol's iodine, aren't safe for people with thyroid conditions. Whoopsie daisy! It's okay, it is just my gland, the one responsible for metabolism, and a variety of other incredibly important jobs, that is slowly dying, no bigguns.

He sold me this little thing to plug into my iPod; I can't remember the *science* behind it, but I bought it, as I felt really vulnerable and desperate. Look, everybody, a health detective cured me with this thing I plug into my iPod. What? Yes. He made it himself and it is most likely magic. If you plug it into your iPod, a message comes on saying, "Hello dummy, thank you for your money!" Actually, it just makes poltergeist white-noise sounds. Maybe it will work for you, though. Fifty dollars, please.

There are plenty of physicians, naturopaths, and qualified people to help a person in my situation. It wasn't worth the gamble to wind up sicker, or disillusioned. In my case, at the end of the "treatment" (or, when I ended it) I felt worse. My thyroid was not working better, even though the energy-measuring machine in his office insisted it was. And it was expensive. I felt embarrassed and angry. Sure, I feel like that most days, but at least in this case I had someone else to direct those feelings towards. That was a nice break. Maybe it wasn't a terrible investment after all.

I also saw an herbalist who was convinced that my thyroid had been crushed in an injury to my neck, and she had a chiropractor who could fix it. Possible, sure. But not the case. Another practitioner told me my condition started when I got pneumonia a few years previous, and another suggested I resolve my issues with my childhood. Hahahaha, what issues?! Another said I needed to voice my opinions more. I assure you, if you knew me, you'd know that wasn't the problem. Give up gluten? Lady, I'd been gluten free for eight years, even before it was cool! I bought so many books, I went to school to study holistic nutrition, I convinced myself I could fix it or I could find a natural way of living with the disease. I took so much advice. I felt like a failure.

One good thing that has changed for me because of this experience is how I listen to people. I try not to offer advice now, even if I might have some. That impulse to find a solution, or to help, can be misguided.

When a dear friend was diagnosed with a very painful and potentially fatal autoimmune disease, I learned to be quiet. Over tea one afternoon she said, "If I don't die in the first two years, I have a really good chance at making it." So maybe I wasn't going to tell her about the article on fish oils, or curcumin, or whatever impulse I had to try to help, or to make it somehow about me. I was just going to sit with my friend in that moment, because I don't have advice for that. I have feeling for that. I have fear and sadness for that. And hope. I have gentle hugs for that. It is okay to not know, and we have to get comfortable in that place of unknowing. And definitely make a lot of fart and/or poop jokes. Always a hit!

Advice is often not support. I would say that cookies are support, but the relationship between foods that cause inflammation and autoimmune disease would suggest otherwise. I know that advice is frequently an expression of frustration and love. But please, don't google someone's condition and offer advice. I have googled it, too. Just laugh with me when I can't tie my shoes, or let me put my cold hands up your shirt. I am going to be fine, even if I never figure it out.

2012

When the summer of 2011 spit me out, I was single and raw from heartbreak. Going through a breakup is awful, going through a breakup unemployed doesn't make it sexier, and going through a breakup unemployed and feeling like you can't wake up and you can't sleep is the most uprooting, hopeless feeling I have had to date. That's sort of how I felt—like a tree, uprooted, lying on the ground, with some green shoots on one side but mostly ravaged by some unknown parasite.

Loss. That will do it. Loss will eat you, like you are a mille feuille pastry—it crushes you in the middle and picks out the parts it likes best, leaving behind just a slip of custard-stained paper.

My energy levels were so low at this point, I only wanted to wear jogging pants (this symptom has never gone away). I went back to my doctor, tail tucked between my legs, where I always keep my tail, so it doesn't get caught in doors. I had read that lots of people with hypothyroidism have success taking desiccated thyroid, and although my doctor was not familiar with it, she wrote me a prescription. I took it to the pharmacy and learned that she had not given me the right prescription but one for another synthetic thyroid medication. As is my way—impatient, annoyed, hungry at all times—I just wanted to start feeling better, so I filled the prescription.

Gradually, I felt better. The worst side effect of this drug was the crying. I cried every day, for many weeks, mostly on walks home from work or on the bus, or when I saw something particularly moving. I cried in the shower, where it was most economical. I tried not to cry over perfectly good acts of kindness made less rewarding by a weirdo crying. Tears came out of nowhere. These tears, on top of the other tears for all of the sadness for myself, really added up. I should have kept a bucket for tear collection, so I could water that tree on the curb.

The drug opened up a well of sensitivity that I cannot close. So if you are telling me about yourself, or you are a beautiful bird, or tree (YOU CAN READ?), then I might cry a bit, but in a cool, you can tell I am good at sex, kind of way.

The best effect of this drug was that it was working. I noticed key factors—one being exercise, and a lot of it—really affected how well I felt. And if I missed a dose, I would feel it, and if I missed two doses, I would feel like I was starting over. Knowing what was a side effect of the drug and what was a reaction to my actual heartache—and the sheer panic of poverty looming while I worked my way through my last year of school—was a real toughie.

But then something lifted in the ruins, and I came out of it. Not like a phoenix from the flame. More like a hot dog that rolled out of the fire into some cool sand. Yeah, a hot dog.

2013

I was finally given the diagnosis of Hashimoto's disease: the reason why my hands are so cold, and why I want to lie down on your couch. Oh, and if you have something sweet, I'd like that, too.

Hashimoto's is an autoimmune disease that damages the thyroid. It has a variety of causes and risk factors, and treatment can vary from person to person—I am no guide in this bleak forest! But for a few years, my symptoms were fairly stable.

And then they weren't.

2015

By March 2015, I had slipped back to a place that was physically and mentally *inconvenient.* And I kept slipping. Stress at work and in my personal life wasn't helping. My Hashimoto's symptoms were back, my thyroid levels were in my boots, and I was almost too tired to care. Sharp pain in my legs woke me up most nights, an all-over stiffness slowed me by the end of each day, and my skin hurt. It what? Yeah, it hurt. My life felt heavy and dark and hopeless.

The most difficult part of 2015 was my parents seeing me in pain. They don't live nearby, so with infrequent visits, my parents hadn't really seen the decline in my health. They were scared, which made me afraid, too. Like when you go to a haunted house and you know it's just a bunch of high school kids dressed up like ghosts, but someone starts screaming, and then you start screaming, too? Yes, exactly like that.

August 4: I spent most of my fortieth birthday in bed, except for when I ate pancakes, twice. I love pancakes. Here is my update on pancakes: I eat them every week. Sometimes for dinner. What? Yes. Sometimes I make a sandwich, but instead of bread, I use pancakes.

In bed that day, full of pancakes, I mustered up a little plan to try something new to feel better, and to keep trying until I found something that worked. That was all I had, but it was something. I couldn't drop out of life any more than I already had. There were squirrels outside that I needed to look at, dogs that needed compliments, and cats that needed to be forcefully pet.

I started by making an appointment with a naturopath. I knew after my first visit that we had similar beliefs about how food and allergies affect autoimmune conditions. I also knew that I needed help, that I wasn't going to be able to do this on my own. I promised myself to be devoted to the process, even though I wasn't optimistic at the time. I was surprised by how quickly things like my weight shifted, but my pain didn't get better for some time. Simple changes. Slow changes. For the first few months, I followed a gentle gut healing protocol. My medication started to work, and the pain in my legs was mostly gone. The absence of pain is a weird and floating feeling. I give it four thumbs-up. Two of those thumbs are actually toes! Gross!

I took a break from drinking and learned a lot about how my body processes alcohol. Turns out: not great! I think I should have done this when I was nineteen, because I was never good at drinking. I promise you that I tried very hard to be good at drinking, and I apologize for the parties I ruined by insisting people arm-wrestle me and for all of the one-handed push-ups I did in restaurants.

I have always liked food that made me forget for a moment that I was uncomfortable in other ways. I would rather have a stomach ache, and maybe some terrible toots, than feel emotions. But when I couldn't eat or drink things that made me forget how I was feeling for a bit, I had to face those feelings. There were some tears in the late part of 2015 that I was unable to soothe with sauerkraut. Hey, there I was with no cookies. And no toots. Weird.

2019

I still struggle with long-ago seeds of unworthiness that rooted in my heart, twisted around my legs, and have taken me down again and again over these forty-three years. Some days I can't push them off. I talk more openly about this now, dragging things out in a way that makes you hug them and let them go, like a cat you know doesn't want to be hugged, but you do it anyway because you are bigger than it is. I talk more openly about this because I think it surprises people that this is part of who I am, and perhaps if they have similar feelings, they won't feel as alone as I have sometimes. Or maybe people are like, *Ew, stop sharing*. Fair. That seems fair.

I try to spend time with people who see me, and I them, for who we are. I will take physical pain over the hurt of not being seen, or not being whole, in the eyes of someone I love. I am trying to bring some softness to my judgment of others as well. Some will always be butt sausages, but I figure a lot of people are having a hard time just getting up—they have their own sadness, their own little voice that keeps them down, or some combination of things that makes them take fifteen minutes to order a coffee while I wait behind them with my brain melting down the front of my face. On good days, I see all these hearts, brains, and bones, getting up and trying.

Lately, I can stay up late and go for long walks and bike rides. I am happy, which feels weird and nice and sexy. I laugh a lot more, and a silliness that had been buried by fatigue has returned and wants to be a brat. Sorry in advance!

When I eat something I shouldn't, or overdo life in some way, and a pain flare starts to build, I climb into bed and wait it out. I am not too proud now to take medication to help. My naturopath taught me about my chronic pain cycle and how to stop it with herbs and over-the-counter pain medicine. I also learned that I can't eat Cheetos, or as I used to call them, party carrots. I stick to a few important diet things—no refined sugar and low grains, lots of vegetables and fruit—plus daily gentle exercise.

This is what has worked best for me in these nine years of figuring it out. Figuring out what works and doesn't for me has already been a lot, so please don't think I can figure anything out for you. Me am no smarts. Me no know. Me like squirrel!

BRAD

I don't know the first time Brad stopped looking at his BlackBerry long enough to notice me. I had noticed him months before, drinking tea at the tiny tiled table at the Granville Island Tea Company. I had *noticed* him. I knew what kind of tea he ordered. I knew that he smelled nice and wore nice things, and he wore them well. I did not feel good about myself, and if I was wearing nice things and someone had said that I wore them well, I would not have believed them.

Brad was handsome, and I was not alone in having a crush on him. As he walked past the vendors in the market, other people would look up to notice him too. But no one else seemed to be planning tea breaks at 11:05 a.m. each weekday to stand next to him, just for a moment, and wonder who he was, besides a man who liked good teas that smelled like smoke or fruit or lavender. The first stage of a crush is strange and voyeuristic and trivializing. Everything the object of affection does is a potential clue or symbol to consider. And I considered all of it, a lot. Like, hey, settle it down, Tobin.

I started taking my lunch at the counter alongside him (yes, a full hour before most people eat lunch, but I will have you know, it is the best time to have lunch precisely because no one else is eating lunch), carefully chewing my carefully chosen food, food that would not spill or leave me with a food moustache (one moustache is enough, thank you). Things that crumbled were fine, because he also ate crumbly things in a self-conscious way: a raspberry scone, or a large cookie or muffin from Muffin Granny, but only if the scones were sold out, perching his fine hands above the white paper pastry bag, silently chewing, while I tried not to notice, or at least not let him notice just how much I was noticing. I do think, just this once in my life, I can say it was love at first sight (just for me). At this point, I had become, and would mostly remain, shy with and hurt by men. Just being around him was nice and, in many ways, nice enough. Just being around someone who makes you feel something without doing anything is highly underrated.

I do remember the difference between not being noticed and being noticed, the moment I went from being invisible and hoping to be noticed to being there. It was a few weeks or months before we spoke. I had ingratiated myself with the staff at the tea shop and come to believe that Brad would not speak to me ever, just a beautiful man who, clearly, everyone loved, who didn't talk to funny women. It is intimidating for unfunny people to try to communicate with hilarious people. I understand. But one day, he did. I felt more alive, my heart beat faster, and my cheeks felt hot as we joked and talked about who even knows what. It didn't matter, and it doesn't matter, but as I write this, I am there, beside him in that warmth.

Over time we became friends, and then he gave me his card, which is funny because cards are dumb and weird and stupid when handed to you by someone you think is cool and you are most likely in love with, but I kept that card at my desk at work for months, flipping it over and wondering, if I had a card, and I had casually given it to him, would he call me? His business card had an illustration of a horse on it. I wondered what I could put on my hypothetical business card and thought a pudding cup might be nice.

Brad would usually ask me what I was doing that weekend, and I would tell him about whatever was the coolest thing I had been invited to (but would never go to because being home is the best and going out is not great). And he would often say, "Maybe we should do something?" But we never did. All of my workmates knew that I loved him and that at eleven a.m. most days I would wander over, at top speed, in a totally nonchalant way, in my best casual but sexy outfit, to see if he was there and if there was room for me, too. Either way, he always made room for me, and I would measure the space between my arm and his arm by the blond hair on mine trying to kiss the blond hair on his.

I always thought that he liked me too, if he wasn't in love with me. Curious, at least, about what it would be like to kiss me—which is great, by the way; I never do anything creepy with my tongue unless we have been dating for a while and I want to make you laugh very hard. Brad once showed up at my place of work on my birthday, sweating, handed me a birthday card, and acted weird about it. A woman at the store said, "That man is in love with you." Regardless of the source, I always shake a card for money first, and when nothing fell out, I read the simple wish: *Happy Birthday, xo Brad.*

So I waited, and saw him on dates with other women, and said encouraging things about life and love, and drank my tea beside him, and memorized his hands, and took note of the things he had a hard time with, to offer advice or to listen and better understand him, and just tried to ignore the crush I had on him.

But one day, I gave up. It had been over a year of waiting, being strung along, with my string responding to the slightest tug of interest, and I was tired of it. I started to see that Brad dated a lot (but not me), and we were just going to be friends, and that was for the best. It wasn't fair of me to pretend to be his friend, either, so I set to the task of really trying to be his friend, for real.

Soon after I made this decision, I met someone lovely, brave, smart, and kind. He was cool, talented, and respectful, and he wanted to hang out with me. I fell in love with him.

And the very next day, it seemed, or as soon as he found out I was in a relationship, Brad took my hand in the market and said he felt like he had missed his chance. I stood silent over my cold premade sushi, my stomach turning with confusion and rage, not just because the salmon rolls were so small and so expensive, but also because I had known it wasn't my imagination, that he had liked me too. I told him it was too late.

But that string was left between my heart and his heart, and over the years, we still met for tea, we talked, and I asked him about dating and work. I really only wanted to know about dating but did my best to express interest in all aspects of his life. Still, I had questions. Why was he alone at forty-one? Was he like my friend's Russian saying about single men in their forties that loosely translates to "a perfectly good sweater that fell behind the dresser and is found a few years later and is still perfectly good even if a bit out of style"? WAS HE A RUSSIAN SWEATER? Or was no one good enough for him? What was the deal?

When things didn't work out with the person I had been dating for many years, my heart wandered back to the fence where I watched Brad. Brad had once told me that we had "unfinished business," and I was curious about that business, as long as it wasn't selling Amway (fool me once, Amway). I survived the grief of my relationship ending by thinking of LIFE: WITH BRAD. I imagined that, somehow, he was my person. It helped me through the loss of that big, important, however-temporary love. I had done this before, and I think it isn't uncommon to focus on something in the distance when your life is burning to the ground. I hoped, as I packed up my stuff and cried myself to sleep, that Brad would still want to go into business with me, the way he had when he took my hand in the market so many years before.

He asked me out immediately. So instead of working through the breakup, I started working on another disaster. I carefully chose a dress that looked very good, a blue one with a white bicycle print, and put yellow vintage barrettes in my hair, and probably looked like a cross between Gilda Radner and another incredibly beautiful and talented woman. Myself? Sure.

For our first date-not-date (take note!) he asked me to join him for some errands, which translated to me as "girlfriend stuff," which was, by the way, ugh, incorrect. I was in school again (holistic nutrition, for people who think food is life-saving but vaccinations aren't) and scraping by with three part-time jobs when Brad took me to south Granville Street to shop. The only thing I could afford there at that time was a discounted candle at Anthropologie, but only if it had a dent in it and smelled like a field of magnolias covered in Monsanto's Roundup. We walked into a store I had only been in once before to ask how much a dog-shaped cookie jar was, and then I passed out and came to and was back in East Vancouver where I belonged. Brad bought sheets that cost $600. They were plain grey with a purple undertone and zero dogs on them. Yes, you heard me right: ZERO DOGS. After he spent what I was earning every two weeks, we went for a drink. Over our two p.m. doubles he told me about his father dying, and he seemed nervous and sad at the same time. He didn't make any of it funny at all! I left thinking that he was a mess and had no idea how much sheets should cost. I was ashamed that I had accepted a date-not-date when I was just a few weeks out of a relationship and got out of his fancy car blocks away from my apartment so that my new roommates wouldn't see.

Months of flirty text exchanges passed before I accepted another date-not-date at his home. I put on my ugliest underpants (trust me) and my nicest clothes and went over to his place in soulless Yaletown. We drank and flirted, and I left before the physical manifestation of my feelings could, y'know, *manifest*, or I had so much to drink that I would forget I was wearing those underpants, which were truly horrible.

Within a few more dates we had PENETRATIVE PENIS VAGINA SEX. It was a lot of buildup, and it was perfect to finally be with him in the way I had started to think about over fancy teas so many years before. I realized that he was one of those men who didn't know where his condoms are (not on his wiener, that's for sure), and I thought it was because he didn't have sex often, but the truth most likely was that he often had sex without a condom. Within a few more days he invited me to meet his friends, and the day after that, while I was still waking up, he had turned cold and I could tell he wanted me to leave his apartment. That is one of the worst feelings, when someone is done with you and you literally just showed up. He had just told me how much he cared for me, and how he had wanted this for so long, but now he was far away, hoping I would leave—and I did.

A few days later, he was texting: I was back in! About a month after we had started sleeping together, he asked me if I had gotten my period, and I said yes, and he said, "Aw, that's too bad. It would be nice to make a baby together," and the floor in the kitchen shifted and I think my uterus tilted (even more) and I held on to the counter. I had an IUD put in the following week.

When people found out we were dating (something I probably let slip any chance I could, to strangers and friends, cashiers, bank tellers, the student loan people, and my parents—oh, here is his picture, oh my gosh, I know, he's so beautiful), it seemed like everyone had a friend who had, or had themselves, been on a date with him. Their stories were eerily similar: they had met, gone on a date, it went great, and they never heard from him again. A mutual friend of a friend cornered me at a party at my house (that he did not show up to) and pumped me for details about him, almost as if to ask how I had gotten a second, third, and ongoing date thing happening with this very aloof man. I sputtered something about how we had been friends for a long time: Our five-year friendship was the foundation of our dating relationship? We understood each other? Maybe? My voice so high the IKEA wine glasses broke.

The weeks went on like this, with me dropping everything to see him, finding time between my part-time jobs and school to make him feel special, to make out with him in his car on my short lunch breaks, to be beside him whenever he made a little room for me. He told me about his mother and the neglect he suffered as a child, and I told him about mine and our problems, and I felt close to him, closer than I had to other men because we were the same in our need for a time machine to repair parts of us that became damaged so early in our lives. It was a relief to be with someone who had not much family and a lot of problems, too. I had felt so much shame in past relationships with men who had happier, closer families. I imagined we would make our own holiday traditions and we could somehow create happiness with our unhappiness. It wasn't science; it was that crushing feeling that children of misery cling to. With each day, I grew more patience for him, I was able to read the storm in his eyes better, and I waited for him to fully let me in, worried that I was not good enough and not the right sort of broken to match his broken pieces. I played it as cool as I could while being absolutely always never cool ever. His friends made fun of him for dating a comedian, and I made fun of his friends for thinking they were cool because they bought a Dyson fan. I mean, I guess they were technically cool in the summer and warm in the winter, and I sometimes look at those fans and dream of having one, too.

The months wore on, with me spending most of my time trying to make plans with Brad and then waiting to hear back from him, checking my phone often, even in the middle of the night. I would invite him to dinner, movies, events, and one night, to meet my best friend, Warren. Brad accepted. Warren bought lovely food and wine, and we waited two hours for him to show up before he cancelled. Still, I left my phone on, in case he reached out.

One night he called, drunk, to tell me I was the only person who understood him and his only true friend, and asked me to come over. The next morning, we made the bed and he said, "I think we are meant to be together, and we will get married. Should we have a kid? C'mon! How great would it be to have a kid?" and my heart said yes, and my brain said no. But still, the thread in my heart, now knotted and dingy and loosely hanging from his, swayed but did not break.

If I told my friends about Brad's emotional treachery, I would have had to end it, and I was not going to lose this horrible love. I kept everything I could in, except the one time I broke down in front of my ex-boyfriend when he asked if I was seeing anyone and all the ugliness I was putting myself through ran down my cheeks and into our vegan dim sum. Slowly, these moments would turn our relationship into a strong and honest friendship. We were not there yet, but having survived so much together already, there was no point in turning back. He told me that Brad didn't sound like a good person and wasn't good for me. I heard him, but I didn't think I deserved anything better.

Brad made plans to move to the United States, and my father said, "If he loved you, he wouldn't make plans without you." So I took my string, so stretched out, with bits of thread falling off, and pulled as much as I could back. I tried to stop contacting him, though I would sleep with him every few weeks and take myself home afterward, lonesome the whole time for my person, who was right there and not letting me in. I helped him shop for his interview clothes; I was his contact on his passport application; I pumped his tires when he wasn't feeling good about himself (I probably would have pumped his actual tires if they'd needed it), which was any time he wasn't drinking; and I hoped he would take me with him when he moved away.

But one night he told me that he had tried to fall in love with me but couldn't, but he still wanted to "date" until he left. And I cried and cried and still slept with him because it felt like it was all I had left for him when I guess it was all he had wanted, and I still wanted him so badly.

And of course, he still wanted to sex me so many times because I am great at sex! It is one of the only ways I can communicate my feelings, and I have so many feelings! But, finally, his ugliness caught up with me that night. I had turned my whole life inside out for the scraps of himself he tossed to me, and I was tired of catching them like a seal at the aquarium.

The day that Brad left Vancouver, a number of photos popped up in my social media feed, of him, his arms wrapped around a beautiful woman while having dinner at a mutual friend's place. The world tilted. I threw up. As he drove away from Vancouver, we argued over the phone. I had asked him outright if he was dating other people and he had promised he wasn't. Don't you dare ask me how many times I have fallen for this. I am not done this essay, but it is more than twice. He was thousands of miles away and I was left in a city where everyone knew one another, and, it soon felt, everyone knew I was a fool. The woman and I had so many friends in common that I became a shut-in, leaving the house only for work and turning down anything where I thought I might bump into people who knew I was a fool and second choice and a desperate loser. I wandered around too embarrassed to be heartbroken. And in his loneliness so far away, Brad would reach out and grab me and twist me, whenever he felt like it. He wrote me in the middle of the night to say he loved me and had made a mistake, and the next day, he would respond to my emails with cold anger. He would say things like *Well, you know I am a little bit of an alcoholic*, or *I am a little bit of a sex addict* that made me feel like horse poop.

One night, after many nights of self-pity, I joked aloud that I would never go outside again because outside is where people are, and people only hurt me. Four minutes later, I walked outside and slipped on a mossy staircase and broke my shoulder. The universe was sending me messages, but I let them go to voice mail. Yet still, I returned his messages, I took his calls, and he took mine. He asked me to come see him on his birthday—he was so *lonely*, had made *no* friends, and wanted to see *me*. I considered it, hard. But the night before I had promised to buy tickets I woke up screaming, "No!"

The night of his birthday he met the woman he would soon marry, and the last time he tried to pull my string she was pregnant with his child. I know we are all broken, in some way. But I will never be as broken as him. It is a special type of broken person who tries to destroy someone else. They try to extinguish a light in others they can't find in themselves. Brad was someone I had not allowed to be a full person either, a character I had created out of a little information and a lot of desire. He had told me a number of times that he wasn't a good person, that he didn't like himself, and that I was too good for him. And I should have believed him.

Now when someone pulls my string, I light up, like an old lamp with no shade that will burn you if you touch it. That light will never go out again.

Also, the last I heard of Brad was that one of those Amazonian fish swam up his wiener and ate it. Wow, eh?

LEARNING TO COOK

Kitchens are the heart of many, but not all, homes. A kitchen's heart beats to the time of egg-shaped timers, scheduled mealtimes, after-school snacks, and the cry of hunger pangs. I spend a lot of time in the kitchen.

My happiest memories as a child are of helping my mother bake. I was given the most important jobs of cleaning batter, icing, and whipped cream bowls and beaters with my mouth, and then washing them as best I could in our sink while wobbling on a vinyl kitchen chair. After that came the waiting, as patiently as possible, for cookies to come out of the oven, banana bread to be sliced and dressed in a smear of thick salted butter, cakes to cool for hours before being iced with sweet chocolate icing. Beside my mother as she baked, true crime shows or talk shows played on a little TV, and she talked to me about life as the kitchen filled with the sweet smells, the anticipation of eating, and the sense of pride I took in my small role in making a dessert that my family would soon enjoy. As a teenager, I started to take a more active role, following handwritten recipes out of my mother's notebook for War Cake, oatmeal cookies, carrot cake with cream cheese icing, or, my favourite, grasshopper pie.

My mother made dinner for us almost every night. Heaping plates of spaghetti Bolognese (we called it spaghetti sauce), Irish stew with steamed dumplings that were a religious experience, French Canadian pea soup with salty undertones of back fat. Horrible nights were Salisbury steak or meat loaf, but I was alone in my campaign against them. Summer we ate baked potatoes loaded with sour cream paired with well-done steaks slathered in HP Sauce, potato salad on a bed of romaine, and bowls of ice cream with store-bought caramel and chocolate sauce topped with crushed salted peanuts. I had a parent who showed her love by feeding us, and when I was a child, my family had money to put food on the table. So when I think about food, when I close my eyes and think about my life and the lives of others, I wish they had this. Except the meat loaf. Unless you want meat loaf, in which case: have mine!

There were a few times in my life when I didn't have money and didn't have a lot of food. The first time was at seventeen, when my mother and I had to go to food banks for a while to make a go of my parents' separation. I was ashamed as my childhood friend Leela helped us load the bags into the back of my mom's car. We had grown up together, and we loved each other, but I felt like we were living in different worlds. The bags of food were so welcome, though. Having had food and then not having food would be a trigger for many years to come. Nothing made me feel as low and alone as an empty fridge or cupboard.

When I was living on my own, I realized I only knew how to bake. I could pour boiling water over Mr. Noodles or microwave something from the freezer section, make pasta (but not sauce) or a tuna salad sandwich. When I was eighteen, possessing bread *and* tuna at the same time was highly unlikely. The first meal I learned to make—keep in mind, this was the mid-1990s, and you had to look up a recipe in a book, or figure it out, as most of us didn't have our own computers and reliable internet yet, and if we did, we weren't looking up recipes—was the fanciest meal I'd had at that point: crab alfredo, which I had tasted at the fanciest restaurant in the world: Red Lobster. The only reason I learned how to make this was to impress a guy. I am not sure that it impressed him, which was good preparation for when I would later lose my virginity to him, which was—how do you say?—not crab-alfredo-level impressive. But I was proud of my linguine! I made a simple dish that tasted almost as good as a Red Lobster meal. I was a natural.

I started to get curious about cooking and read second-hand *Martha Stewart Living* magazines and bought fancier cans of soup. Montreal was the best place to be broke and hungry. Everyone is always talking about food, and there's great food at any and every price: crispy falafel, goat roti, thick hamburgers spiced with za'atar, injera with lentil stew, chicken tikka masala and warm naan, poutine, souvlaki, and seven-dollar steak frites. Fresh bagels out of a paper bag? Heaven. Montreal is the place to be if you need cheap food and you like it all. And I did. When I was nineteen or so, a few friends of mine worked as busboys at an upscale restaurant, and we would go there after work to drink and, on occasion, eat. I still remember, and always will, the first time I tried meat that wasn't well done. I felt strange, seeing the pink piece of veal being offered to me on the end of a fork, and tried not to hear my mother's voice in the background—the voice of a woman who sent hamburgers back at McDonald's because they were underdone—yelling, "Don't eat uncooked meat or you will die!" I ate it. It brought tears to my eyes. Later, when I learned how veal is raised, the tears were for different reasons, different essays.

One of the nicest gifts I ever received was a new set of pots and pans from my mother, a set of matching dishes from my childhood, and a second-hand table she found for me at a garage sale. Nothing made me want to cook more than the space and tools to do so. I opened up an inner world where I could put down the abrasive and defensive personality I curated in my late teens and start loving people in a way I knew. Not through words but through service, through cooking, and laughing and drinking. I never belong more, I never feel more like part of a family than when I am able to share food, especially my food, with people. The distraction of creating and cooking gives me little time to overthink conversations. My hands are busy; my mind is calm.

When I think of the most romantic gestures I have received, I think of a suitor showing up at work with a fresh panino of cheddar and green apple, or a gift of a black plum, or a handful of fresh shiitake mushrooms. There is no ring on this finger, but if there were, it would be made of chives.

Until I was twenty-five or so, when paycheques disappeared so fast, it wasn't unusual for me to scrape by on five dollars a day until payday, living on eggs, apples, and noodles. When payday did arrive, it was always about food. When I would run out of food, not money, was when I would panic. It was the hardest low I know. I always had friends and family to help me if I ever needed some money for groceries or to be treated to a meal I would soon pay back, but that connection between food and stability that rocked me in my youth still clung to me—and I know that we had it better than many. I longed for days when I wasn't always worried about food, but just around the time that life started to become stable, something shifted, as it always does. That carrot of stability, that stretch of normalcy, seems to be the big joke in life. It never really endures.

When I was thirty, I found out I was allergic to gluten and was forced to see food and community differently. I felt like I had been benched in the game of life. The things I was good at—eating and cooking—were suddenly gone. So were the crushing cramps, though. So, there was that.

I could no longer simply eat out, and I had to learn to cook rice for the first time in my life (I mean, rice that wasn't risotto). It was humbling. It was grounding. And it was bullshit. I miss bagels, good pizza, bad pizza. I mourn dim sum, long for naan, warm pita dipped in taramosalata, and sometimes just a bowl of my favourite cereal or pancakes at a restaurant. The whole dining-out experience has changed for me. It has become more about finding something worry-free to eat and soaking up the social time with friends, which to be honest, isn't as good as a heaping plate of Red Lobster crab alfredo. But it is close.

THE PAINTED HOUSE

I step over the painting supplies for the seventh day in a row and climb the stairs to my apartment. The house is old, built in 1911 and converted to four suites at some point, and is now getting dolled up to be put onto the hottest real estate market in Canada. Sure, the house needs a new roof, but this coat of paint is like putting red lipstick on a tired face: instant improvement. When the house is finished being painted, the yard will be punctuated by a red-and-blue For Sale sign. I knew this day would come. I knew it was too good to last. A dog-friendly apartment in a nice house, with great landlords and neighbours? In Vancouver? You've got to be shitting me.

The house is being repainted the same colour—forest green with a soft yellow trim—and she looks good. The house sits on a little hill, so when you drive up from crowded 12th Avenue, she lights up the dreary street. People always stop me to ask questions about it, and I immediately explain that I rent, do not own, this house. Who owns a house in Vancouver? Certainly not a single woman, a creative type, with less than $1,000 in her Registered Retirement Savings Plan and an accident-prone poodle. The house will be put up for sale in the coming weeks, and I will face what all renters in Vancouver dread: finding an affordable place to live that isn't a sopping-wet basement suite. Every day

I hope the painters stop painting so quickly and so well and so politely. "Paint over the windows!" I want to shout. "Excuse me please, but could you write 'fuck you' on the doors, if you don't mind, kind sir?!" But we just exchange smiles, and Hank the poodle soaks up their attention. I want to hate them and their work, but it is perfect. Finally, the painters finish. The For Sale sign goes up, and my hopes crash. This is the longest I have lived in any apartment in Vancouver. Three years.

Unlike Montreal, where there are still deals to be found on beautiful, bright, huge apartments, Vancouver tends to be less of a renter's paradise. My last place was an expensive basement suite (advertised as a "garden suite") with hardly any natural light, even in the middle of summer, and kind but serious landlords who built the apartment as a little income unit to help with retirement.

The apartment before that was a room in a large house I shared with a few friends, in a time of transition between the end of a long-term relationship and a late return to school, while working three part-time jobs to survive. The downstairs unit was prone to parties that started at two a.m. and ended just about the time I needed to go to work, which was thoughtful of them. Our landlord was hands-off, which is great when you are twenty but felt incredibly irresponsible when I took a hard fall down a flight of poorly maintained, slimy, moss-covered stairs and broke my shoulder in the middle of a dark rainy night.

The apartment before that was what is charmingly called an illegal suite, so, as you can imagine, getting anything fixed there was unlikely. The house was maintained by a lovely and kind hunchbacked eighty-year-old who traded his services for a tiny room in the dreary basement that he shared with a man who was obsessed with radios. One weekend,

I left for a few days and angry crows moved into the eaves but promptly left the first time the faucets stopped working, which was every other day, it seemed.

Before that, I had a beautiful apartment on Cambie Street, with perfectly preserved tile and hardwood from the 1950s, where I didn't sleep for a full year because at night Cambie becomes a makeshift highway for transport trucks. By the way, Vancouver has no real highways. Great planning!

When the place before became infested with mice, a crusty landlord dropped off a few mousetraps in a paper bag and wished us luck. You may be thinking I just rent cheap places, but all of those were expensive, I swear it. Vancouver is just a city where property owners take advantage of renters. There is a stark contrast here between people who own their home and those who don't.

My very first Vancouver apartment I shared with my friend Shane, my first out gay friend and a treasure. It was on Davie Street in the West End. The carpet was from sometime in the late 1970s and always felt damp from the sea air that blew in through the cracks in the cheap single-paned windows. Shane would often say the best part about the apartment was that bread would never go stale, but I noticed it would get mouldy very quickly! Black mould bit at the edges of the bathroom, the old tiles a battleground against their shadow. We lived a ten-minute walk from the beach at English Bay, and we would walk down there often to explore Stanley Park. My friend Steven would joyfully jump on the discarded packets of lubricant we would find on the trails, squeezing out the remaining bit as we squealed with laughter. There is so much beauty here! Gross!

Every apartment has a story, and so rarely in Vancouver is that story a good one. So I have cherished my current place for the past few years. Finally, a place that is mine. A pied-à-terre for my world-weary body. I love this house, and my corner of it is home. I have been so at peace here and so safe in my unhappiness, in my tree house. I painted it white, so my colourful art and furnishings could really shine. I decorated it with things I love: a few good pieces of teak furniture I bought with money earned from either stand-up or writing, gifts from my parents, and special objects from local artists, people I know and love and want to be like.

When I walk up the street and lay eyes on this old place, my heart expands. I know all my neighbours and have a key to a few of their homes to check in on beloved pets or take in mail and water plants. I have at last found my city. I say hello to everyone, except Firework Dad, a motorcycle enthusiast who is obsessed with the one day a year fireworks are legal in Vancouver (Halloween) and sets off Roman candles for seven hours until I break down and scream at him and his children. No hellos for you, sir! But apart from that guy, and a handful of other turd hats and hot-dog heads, I really try to connect with most of my neighbours and make this little corner of Fraserhood home. And it is. People know my dog, Hank, who happily approaches everyone with the kind of enthusiasm a pug would be embarrassed by. I cherish the parishioners of the Russian church next door, some new to Canada, their choir rousing me from sleep during their midnight masses. I help out and am helped out by my community. I am on coyote watch and make sure parents and pet owners know when one is nearby (hint: always). Sometimes one is so close I can watch it eat whatever slower animal it found.

It is unnerving to live in a city that is always at odds with nature, where bears surf garbage trucks right into the downtown core (true story!), where raccoons occasionally attack humans and feed on small dogs. Bald eagles? Heck, I have met a few, and the screeching chicks of a Cooper's hawk, none of whom would survive the constant cruel attacks of a murder of crows. I had to stop walking near my workplace for a while because of a cougar sighting in the park. Each day is like a perfect Neko Case song (well, I mean, all Neko Case songs are perfect and somehow push and pull modern living against the naked truth of a wild and more powerful world). I never had to worry in Montreal that I would be killed by a cougar in my business casuals.

I say this with humble pride: I feel like I am adding something to the culture of Vancouver. My comedy shows and podcasts highlight some of the best and brightest local comedians and artists. I finally feel like Vancouver is my town. It isn't perfect, and it often isn't nice, but I fought to make it out here and can cope with the long wet winters and the cold exterior of so many of the inhabitants that breaks with any small gesture of kindness and warms up instantly at human connection. It is too late to move, but it is so difficult to stay. I have so many good friends here. Just four, but I know, still, four good friends is to be truly spoiled. I am, in terms of friends, a wealthy person.

I look out my window: the late-spring cherry blossoms sagging in the heat, the mountains rising up behind them like black sesame soft serve. Almost every street in Vancouver is lined with cherry trees, and deep reddish-pink to bright white blooms spray-paint the air. No one can resist taking a picture of the trees to capture this time of year. Tourists risk being mowed down standing in the middle of the street to get photos of these huge pink pompoms. I reach over my big mossy balcony and cut a few off and put them in a jar on my coffee table. At my first job in Montreal, I worked at a florist selling greens that grow on the West Coast all year round. I think about the few beach days I will manage this summer and feel happy.

In the first week on the market, the house doesn't sell, which is strange. Everything sells in a week in Canada's hottest real estate market. I use an online mortgage calculator to guesstimate what the new owner would have to pay each month if they decided to keep the current tenants. The house is selling for $2.3 million, and deducting our rents from the mortgage, the new owner would have to pay about $5,000 a month for the small three-bedroom suite they could occupy. I start to doubt anyone who buys the house will be the kind of person who will also want to live here. We are now living in what is called an investment property and the buyers will be investors. I don't really know what that means, but I hope we get another lovely family with children downstairs, similar to the current landlords. Something just doesn't feel right when seniors or children aren't around to remind us who we were and who we will be.

Neighbours have already started asking me what I'm going to do, but they are asking in the removed way that people who own houses can. I try to be polite, but I don't know what I'm going to do or where I'm going to go if I get evicted. Pet-friendly housing is almost non-existent in Vancouver—a man I know who was renovicted rejoiced when he found a basement suite for $1,850 a month, which is double what I pay and about $300 more than I can manage. I don't want to live in a basement ever again, but it seems to be the most common option if one gets lucky enough to find a pet-friendly apartment. People are forced to abandon their pets to shelters or live on the streets with them. It also isn't unusual to see people who are recently homeless sleeping in the parks in tents or in their cars. Major streets like Robson, once the bustling retail dream, are lined with homeless people occupying the doorways of the abandoned storefronts, with sleeping bags, bottles of water, a cherished dog spooning them for warmth. Even the storefront where I first worked when I moved here twenty years ago is now an open-concept bachelor with concrete floors. Not even massive retail giants like the Gap can pay rent here. Robson Street is dead.

I am forty-three. I should be saving and planning and starting to enjoy life a bit more, but I feel helpless and angry. The other tenants in the house feel the same way. On the verge of forced and unwanted change, we wait out each viewing of the house and hope someone nice doesn't use one of the few loopholes left to push us out.

The real estate agent reminds me of Biff from the *Back to the Future* movies. Biff always sends a text message a day before he shows the house and calls the apartments our homes, but it doesn't ring true. Each time I come "home" after a showing, I can see someone has been sitting on my bed, and I feel a bit violated. I don't smooth out my duvet cover each morning to have a small sense of order and control over my world just to have someone's weird butt indent on it after a long day at work! When I find out it is Biff who is lounging on my furniture, I know that he doesn't think of this as my home. I make sure to never be around for showings, often waiting down the street until the last Lexus or BMW leaves.

One day, though, I happen to cross paths with Biff and a potential buyer. I had spent the late afternoon at the vet after my dog, really still a puppy, ate some marijuana he must have found on his walk. Pot is everywhere here; each corner of each neighbourhood has a store to sell you some weed to help you cope with life on the Best Coast. Unfortunately, it is incredibly toxic to animals, and my miniature poodle was now completely gooned. I was exhausted but grateful he would be fine in eighteen hours and desperate to get into my place to rest. I held Hank in my arms a few feet away while I waited for the agent and the client to leave, but they didn't. They spoke in animated tones about the market, and as I stood at the foot of the stairs, they quipped about how easy it will be to evict all of us. I pushed past them, stoned dog in my arms, and went into my apartment that no longer felt like home.

The showings continued, offers fell through, and the market ground to a halt. Other equally beautiful homes were not selling, not in the first week, not in the first month, and not at all. I felt bad for my landlords, who were also friends. As much as I wanted to stay, I also wanted them to have a fresh start in the new home they had built ten minutes away. I tried to focus on how grateful I was for having had this place at all, and to let go of it.

October 2018. The house is still unsold. My friends have moved out and a family of squirrels has moved in. I know it's a family, maybe a single mom, because she is frenzied finding food, her milky squirrel teats swinging beneath her agile frame. I can't lie, I love squirrels (yes, I said milky squirrel teats in a positive way, because, yes, I love everything about squirrels), but I know they're bad tenants. Everyone—well, maybe mostly just me, and everyone else backs off because I am a bit weird about animals—decides to let the squirrels get a bit bigger before renovicting them. Give the mother a chance to raise her babies in a safe place for a few weeks. This is a mistake for a few reasons, one being that nursing squirrels are very territorial and my dog's biggest dream in life is to eat a squirrel. The balcony becomes a battleground for screaming squirrel and barking dog until the wildlife specialist (exterminator) installs a one-way door and the squirrel family moves on.

New neighbours, human neighbours, move in downstairs, a group of women who love their new, affordable apartment with a tiny backyard garden and nice upstairs neighbours who also care about where they live. A new era begins in the green house with the yellow trim. I start to fall in love with my place again, do a little sprucing up, and erase the memories of Biff and his butt imprints. I cautiously make it home again, and I wait and watch the snow gather on the mountains and melt again.

At the end of February, I get the message: the house will be put back up for sale. I brace myself for more Biff, and the house sells on the first showing. At the end of March 2019, as I write this, we are told we are getting evicted. It feels at once like a long time coming and a swift punch in the guts. Here I am, one of many, who chose Vancouver as home but can't seem to find one here.

CHRISTMAS

It is November 22 and I have already started to worry about Christmas. I am worried about all of the discussions I am going to have to have about eggnog. I don't like eggs in my nog. I mean, eggnog has all the elements I normally like—nutmeg, milk, eggs, booze—but it feels like a drink from another time that should have stayed there, the place where people died from consuming spoiled egg drinks all the time. Can you imagine what it was like to add a raw egg to something in hopes of improving it? Yuck. I also worry about gift giving, in a pathological way, and make myself sick trying to get just the right thing for people I love to prove that I love them, which they already know, but what if they don't? And lastly, I'm anxious about THE HOLIDAYS.

As a non-practising Christian, to me Christmas pretty much means what it meant when I was six: lights, chocolates, tree, and carols. And deep uncertainty and a feeling of helplessness. I guess around that age it became clear that Christmas Never Works Out. And No Matter How Much I Do, No One Is Happy. I already knew that Santa wasn't real and felt a rare superiority to other children who did not know yet, while secretly wishing he was real because the odds Santa would gift me a small horse and a Canadian Tire shed to keep him in seemed higher than convincing my parents. I had already tried that, pretty much every time my parents went to Canadian Tire. For the uninitiated, Canadian Tire is a store with terrible customer service but very good prices, so it is perfect for Canadians. It's also pretty much the only place where you can buy a hunting rifle (which is what Canadians have to use if they want to kill someone) or a casserole dish, get your car tuned up, and find a good snow shovel. You *could* also buy a reasonably-sized shed that could easily be repurposed for a small horse barn and placed either beside the house or in the backyard. MOM, DAD, ARE YOU LISTENING? LET'S MAKE A DEAL!

This year, I got my parents Christmas cards. Cards mean a lot to both my parents, but it turns out that cards are not enough to keep a marriage together. Hey Hallmark, you suck. Over the years, I have learned to ignore the side of me that wants to buy a sweet, locally made card with a hand-drawn bear on the front wearing a wreath that simply reads, *The Holidays Are Unbearable* and instead go to the card store and sift through the lavishly priced Christmas cards, getting glittered, getting Jingle Bell Rocked, getting fleeced, and reading carefully through each card to find one that doesn't mention that childhood was very hard, that my parents weren't meant to be married, and that my brother and I struggle as adults with that pain. I find one with cheerful animals on the front, and a $9.99 price tag on the back, that says something true about being happy that someone is in our life. And I am happy I still have my mom.

My mom is a beautiful person. I can remember her joy when I was small, the way her breath smelled like half a chew of Trident gum and faintly of cigarettes. Sweet and truly comforting, mixed with her soapy perfume. She was tall and languid, with high cheekbones and sharp blue eyes. I remember beaming with pride when, she stepped out of her silver Camaro wearing her rabbit-fur coat (in the winter in Quebec, with six-foot snowbanks framing her, this was truly something), her blond hair always perfect, her nails long and lacquered, to take my brother and me home for lunch. She was so striking, so funny, and so unlike any other mother in that parking lot. My brother and I would pile into the car, and I would climb into the back seat to save myself from being punched out of my older brother's rightful spot. I would look at my mother and brother and wish we didn't have to go back to school after lunch and could instead walk our big collie, Prince, and then dance to the *Star Wars* soundtrack (you better believe it when I tell you that Prince danced, too) or listen to the comedy albums she loved or make a fort together and put on Tchaikovsky's *Peter and the Wolf* while blowing on hot chocolate and munching Jiffy Pop. She was one of us at that time: young, and full of love.

We lived in a big house, which was unusual for two adults who came from little with lots of baggage. My dad lost his father when he was just eleven; his dad collapsed while they were gardening together and did not survive the heart attack he suffered at forty-two. My father was raised by his mother. He was a poor child on scholarship at Stanstead College, where he struggled to fit in with the children of wealthy parents (or, if we're being generous, maybe they didn't fit in with him). He never finished university, and never realized his dream of becoming a race car driver, so, like most of us who don't have a clear path in life, he got into sales and traded in his youth and partying for a stable job to support his wife and family.

My mom was born on the East Coast. Her mother was an Irish Canadian orphan who was put up for adoption when her parents divorced. They didn't even die! Holy shit, life was so harsh in olden times! The family that adopted Grammy used her as cheap labour, and when it was her turn to have a family, she was a devoted and selfless parent. My grandfather was a carpenter who was happy to make cabinets but found there was more money in caskets, so my mother spent her entire childhood in a funeral home. My grandfather and grandmother ran the family business, and my mother and aunts and uncle all chipped in as they grew. First, my mother was charged with polishing her father's shoes for funerals, then doing the makeup and hair on the corpses (makeup artist for the beyond!), and finally, driving the hearse by the time she was fifteen. Everyone had a job, but most of the work fell onto the shoulders of my grandmother. My grandfather, suffering most likely from bipolar disorder, would swing from highs when he would spend all of the family's money to lows when he locked himself in the attic for weeks, un-showered, or the worst, when he misfired his gun and instead of losing his life in the woods that day, he just made his face look funny. Mental illness was not spoken about or treated. Families and individuals suffered and self-medicated and survived, if they could. Children were also not children back then but small adults. They were the creations of people who survived world wars and depressions and immigration and polio. Female children were even less children than boys and, collectively, so easily preyed upon. My mother never had it easy, and as soon as she could leave, she did, for Montreal, where she eventually met my father.

I knew something was wrong when the yelling started and didn't seem to stop. My father will never play the hero in my childhood, and my mother will never be the villain, but something was terribly wrong in the marriage, and with my mother's coping skills. If my father came home late from work, he would be met with jealous rage. My brother and I would sometimes hide in the garage to wait it out with our collie and a bag of ripple chips or cheese crackers, sipping no-name root beer. We were so small. We internalized these arguments differently: I would do anything to please my mom and stay on her good side, and my brother rebelled, becoming angry and frustrated. Neither of us really knew who we would be coming home to on any given day: Mom who dances with us, Mom who locked herself in the bedroom, or Mom who could tear us down with just one comment. Children adapt to their environment, as they have no other choice.

My father became increasingly less available to us. They separated soon after. He showed us around his sparse apartment in Pointe-Claire, with the single folding bed from our spare room, and I could feel that he was peaceful there and I knew he might never come home. But he did, and the cycle continued, and escalated.

One afternoon, I returned home and the ambulance was outside. My mom was being lifted down the stairs on a stretcher and crying, "I couldn't go through with it. I could never leave you children," or something else that trauma has reworded over time. I think of this day as the moment I started to develop my very cool and very attractive fear of abandonment. PLEASE DON'T PUT THE BOOK DOWN! I can remember a lot of that day. It was the first time I knew of when other adults saw what went on in our home, and I felt deep fear and shame. Our neighbour Kay took me in that night and often after that, just for quiet time. She would set me up in front of the TV with dinner or store-bought gingersnaps. I still seek out those cookies on bad days, as they are so crunchy a person can barely hear their own destructive thoughts.

Christmas that year, and each year after that I can remember, consisted of diminishing attempts to be happy for one or two days. The pressure of parenthood and unhappy family life, my mother's need to argue and then make up so that she could feel something, would usually start early in the day. She might ask if I was "going to poke my face full of chocolate all day" (the answer was yes, but now I would do it in private, thank you very much). Or she might tell me to smile, because so many children had nothing. I didn't care about those kids then, but I felt guilty for feeling like something was missing. And something *was* missing: the Care Bear I had specifically asked for.

One November, Mom simply wasn't home when we got back from school. She'd left us and gone back to New Brunswick. I would call her after school, after days of hiding how alone I felt, and cry until I couldn't breathe while begging her to come home. Because even though our family life was hard, I couldn't think of a life without her. She came home just before Christmas, and I remember she asked my dad for a new hair dryer for her gift. I was so excited when she opened her new hair dryer and so shocked when she was upset and disappointed by it. I would never know the rules of this game and try to be benched as often as possible. My parents would stay together until I was almost eighteen.

It is a rainy November 22, and I take the bus back to East Vancouver with an expensive, pretty, sweet, and vague card in my bag, and I start to feel overwhelmed by all the blank space on it. In better years, when my mom and I were speaking and able to push down our barriers a bit and hold hands over the fences we built to protect ourselves from each other, and also, ironically, ourselves, filling in this blank space on a card would have been easier. Now, I don't know what to write in that space.

What I want to write is that I see how much you have suffered, Mom. I see how hard it all was. I wish there had been help for you, and for us. And I can't forgive you, because there is nothing to forgive. And thank you for dancing with me. For making me funny and kind, for teaching me to speak up against injustice, to—no matter how down I feel—get in the shower and put on some blush, no, wait, that is too much blush, that is clown blush. You were a good parent in ways so few are. And I can't not have you in my life.

I emailed her this morning with the subject line *Checking In*. It has been four months since we last spoke. Not our longest pause, but with her fragile health and advancing age, it has been a stress. A very guilty stress, as this time it was my own doing after catching her in a lie. Tears freely stream down my face on the bus ride home from the card shop. I mean, if you are going to cry anywhere in public, do it on the bus; it is a can of shared human misery and smells. Still, in my heart, as she was when I was six, is the woman who loved me as best she could, with all she had.

I notice as I walk home people are decorating early: sprays and sprangles (this is a word I just made up that legally contributes to the word count of this essay) of LED lights are woven through the empty branches of cherry trees, gingko trees, monkey puzzle trees, and other trees that probably also have names, but I only use the internet for sad news. The new-millennium, we-ruined-the-earth lights don't really illuminate anything, but they make the grey of November thicker and warmer somehow. I miss the "real" lights that ruined the earth, but I am happy that anyone tries, really. It doesn't feel good to celebrate parts of a holiday that promote divisiveness, colonialism, and capitalism, and leave so many people feeling alone and unloved, or even just annoyed at helpless reindeer with birth defects. It seems like people are putting up trees early, too. I see little cozy vignettes in living rooms; a father lifting his child up to put a star on the tree almost overwhelms me with emotion as my body ovulates hard because the dad is handsome, while my brain recoils from glimpsing such a private and precious moment.

There are a couple reasons people could be decorating early: maybe they misread the calendar and think it's actually December, or perhaps the vulgarity of Black Friday and Cyber Monday deals ushered in a sense of urgency around the holidays. But I think it's because they need it. Christmas is not an easy time for anyone, and people need some brightness and something to look forward to. Anything with a bit of hope. In two days, the United States will tear-gas helpless women, men, and children simply looking for a new start, a place to stay. It is another ugly year. So, lights, trees, anything bright. Booze! Drugs! Loose men or women or non-binary people, let's all just, ugh, I don't know, hug?

I find myself at a mall on the following Monday, returning pants that did fit but not well, and on my way back to the SkyTrain I wander into the Bay. All of the ornaments in the department store are on sale. I look for a tree topper and the only one is an angel with a confused face. I consider her for a few moments; one of her hands seems to be raised to give an awkward high-five, but her eyes look afraid. She was probably trying to high-five Jesus, but he didn't notice, so she brushed her hair back as though she had never intended to high-five the Lord, and then he turned her into a tree topper. I put the angel down and think that for sure I want an angel for my tree and wonder what happened to the one we had as kids. She was made of thin plastic with a small light in the back. She looked peaceful with her halo of tinsel. I want that angel so desperately.

The best part of the holiday when I was small was Christmas Eve. My mother would pull out an old 8-track and the Christmas tapes she had found in a bin at K-Mart. Our favourite was *A Gene Autry Christmas*. The tape was already damaged the day we bought it, and midway through "Rudolph the Red-Nosed Reindeer," it would repeat, and we would laugh and sing all the mistakes with great gusto. Even after my parents divorced, even the year that our Christmas groceries came from the food bank, we played that tape and laughed. I can't look back on my life and not remember how much work it all must have been for my mom. To try to make a sad family happy. An unhappy marriage whole. I think of my mom each day and wish I could remember each time she showed me her powerful love instead of the pain I am sure we are both feeling tonight in the glow of our lonesome Christmas trees.

THREE DOGS

There have always been dogs in my life—well, almost always. My first dog was Prince, a huge Scotch collie, or as people would say, a Lassie dog. There's a picture of Prince, my brother, my mother, and me in the late 1970s with a huge green car in the background. Prince and I were just puppies; he still had his fluffy baby fur, and I still had my fluffy red hair that would eventually turn black with age and, I'm guessing, bitterness.

Prince was a beautiful dog. Iconic because of Hollywood and adored because he was calm, obedient, and loyal. A dog who set the standard far too high for any other dog: Prince never needed a leash, and if he walked with one, it always made a lazy U shape between the walker and the walked. He would keep a watchful eye on my brother and me when we were small and herd us back onto the lawn if we wandered too far. Like many children, I felt alone in the world, and different and scared, so having a big dog I could lie against while I read books or bury my face in his huge mane and cry when my feelings were hurt or hang out with when my parents argued was ... better than not that? Like children, dogs don't choose their families, so they make the best of it and play a role that is sometimes more burden than bliss. He kept us all feeling loved when we felt unlovable. Pets do that. It is the deepest act of service: they accept us when no one else does, especially ourselves.

Family lore has it that Prince suffered a terrible injury when he was just a young dog; my dad accidentally slammed his tail in a door and hurt him so severely that his tailbone was exposed. My parents rushed him to the vet, worried his tail would have to be amputated, but the vet reached down and pulled a bright pink Velcro hair roller out of his tail fur that wasn't exposed bone after all. Tobins? Yeah, we know how to party.

Prince was my mother's constant companion during the lonely days of raising two children. He was my father's pride, and the only one of his dependents who could catch a ball. And he was my brother's adventure scout and my secret-keeper; for a lonely child with few friends, he was number one.

When Prince died, our family started to really fall apart. That dog held us together. He was just nine, and I was eleven and had lost one of my only two friends. We buried him like a Pharaoh, with all of his possessions for an afterlife, we hoped, of ball chasing and squirrel eating, which he wasn't allowed to do on Earth. We were all heartbroken. That dog was so good to us.

When I was about twenty-one, I inherited a dog through a friend, who was given the dog as a gift, by someone who had a crush on her. I remember seeing the puppy and, strangely, somehow knowing that dog would be mine. He was a small black lab mix, cradled in her arms. She had brought him to a play, it was *Troilus and Cressida*, and the puppy and I slept the entire time. I would have probably called him Pizza or Inky, but she called him Troy. After many months of trying to care for the puppy and be a full-time student, she offered me Troy, and I took him on the condition that if we didn't get along, she would take him back. After two full weeks of definitely not getting along—my apartment was in a shambles, my favourite watch had been eaten, and Troy was beside himself with the grief of abandonment—I called my "friend" and left a message to come pick up the dog.

She never called me back! I am so glad she didn't, and if you ever read this, Ilona, thank you.

Troy was a wonderful, anxious dog. I tried to change his name to Troika, to Tron, to anything but Troy, which sounded more like a gas station attendant than Shakespeare. But Troy was Troy. He wasn't a confident dog, but he was gentle, silly, sweet, and prone to destruction when left alone. Each day, coming home from my job selling plants and making bouquets in Old Montreal, I would hold my breath as I pushed open the door to the fire-trap loft I shared with two friends, hoping Troy hadn't eaten something irreplaceable. Rarely would Troy have survived the day without shredding something that belonged to me or one of my patient, Troy-loving roommates. He unpotted and tore apart houseplants, pushed over furniture, eviscerated the garbage, ate socks, and pulled plates off the counter. I had only ever had a dog that my parents had trained. I had no idea that Troy was suffering from separation anxiety, and I didn't have the money for a dog trainer.

There was a lot of yelling in those early months, but eventually, I figured out how to Troy-proof the apartment and started taking him to work with me most days. I did the long walk from the Plateau to Old Montreal twice a day all year long with a lanky dog desperate to eat garbage beside me. Troy had been very well trained before he was given to me, and could walk off leash beside me, as long as there was no food anywhere. But we lived in Montreal—there is food everywhere—and we lived in the Plateau—it was party town in the 1990s, lined with cheap pizza places, falafel joints, and schnitzel stands, and if Troy spotted a triangle of discarded pizza, he was gone. He could Houdini out of his harness to run into the middle of Saint Laurent and swallow the slice whole.

Troy wasn't a perfect dog, but he was a perfect friend. I could take him everywhere that allowed dogs, and to a few places that didn't. Troy had a sweetness I have rarely encountered in anyone, and he was humble (in a doggish way) and always looked like he was wearing a rumpled tuxedo. He fit in. He was loved by everyone. He was the kind of dog that made you feel good. Friends who had grown up afraid of dogs soon grew to trust and love him—he was a gateway dog, teaching people who had reasonable fears of dogs that this blockhead mutt was gentle and sweet. Troy travelled with me to the West Coast and made it feel like home. He grounded me in the years of heartbreak and growth that could have unhinged me. He reminded me to get up and get out and be in the world. He also taught me that a dog can eat a belt, a watch, a dozen dirty diapers, and survive.

When a man I was dating locked me out of our apartment and hit Troy for sneaking away on garbage day and doing what Troy did (eat garbage with abandon), I got a wake-up call I really needed. I planned how to leave that man. No one hits my dog. I found out later that man hit women, too. Troy and I never looked back.

Our next few years together, I spent almost all of my time just becoming more of myself, and Troy grew grey and softer, ate less garbage, and slept more. When I moved back to Montreal in 2004, he made that trip, too, reuniting with many old friends. I thought moving home was the best idea after giving Vancouver a half-hearted try for five years. I had planned to finish my BA in psychology at Concordia and work part time, but nothing seemed to be working out. I hadn't applied for student loans properly and had to drop out. I was broke. I could barely afford dog, or any other kind of, food. So I decided to move back to Vancouver. It was crazy: I had just gotten home, but home wasn't home anymore. I remember looking at the shambles of my life and looking at Troy and thinking, *Thank God I still have my dog.*

And then, suddenly, at the end of what I call my country-song year, a few weeks before I planned to fly what I had left back to Vancouver, Troy became sick, and he wasn't going to get better. I had promised myself when I got him that I would not let him suffer, and I made his last few days as love-filled as possible. We had our favourite burger. I lay on the floor with him. I cried into his fur. I told him all the things you should always tell a dog: that you are good, that you mean the world to me, and that you smell like Doritos. At two a.m., he had a stroke and my friend Meeta and I took him to Emergency. I went to a small room with Troy and a vet came in and confirmed it was time. Everything was spinning. Troy seemed almost fine, but I couldn't breathe. They gave him something to relax him, and then the medication that would ease him into death. I watched him slip away: my friend. And when he was gone, he was gone. I don't think I have ever been so alone as when I left that room. I was so broke I had to wake up my father in Portland to pay the vet. Troy was nine, and after that year, I think I was 100.

Troy was with me through the hardest, most insecure time in my life. I cried every day for a year after he died. I wished I'd had more time, longer walks, a vacation to take him on (oh no—I am crying as

I write this). For years after his death, I would dream that he was alive and then wake up to an empty house. I still sometimes catch my breath when I see the ubiquitous black lab mixes that dot my neighbourhood and believe in my whole heart of hearts all Troy dogs are the best dogs.

I caution younger people about getting a dog when they could be out having adventures, travelling, and learning about the world. A dog will hold you back from travelling, but a dog will also teach you, in many ways, exactly who you are and, hopefully, how to be a better version of yourself. Maybe going to Japan will do that for you too, but I am glad I had Troy. Maybe it seems strange to credit a forty-five-pound pit bull/lab for the better parts of my personality, but there it is. He taught me that he was worth something, and he taught me that I was worth something. He showed me that animals are real, too, deserving of respect, understanding, protection, and kindness. Also, Troy once ate a pair of children's underpants filled with frozen poop and then threw them up about eight hours later, so he also taught me ... I don't know ... to never give up on who you are? Even if you are a gross, weird dog who has no idea what is food and what isn't?

I moved back to Vancouver without Troy. Without a job. Without much hope. But things were easier in other areas. I had friends and, in a few months, a pretty good job. I started to do life a lot more differently, and, yes, eventually, I thought about getting another dog. I volunteered at the city pound and eyed up the new dogs, took them for a spin, watched happy people leave with new pets, but it didn't feel right. There is no replacing anyone, and with many aspects of life, I am slow to heal. I also had a different life: I had more responsibility and a boyfriend who was allergic to dogs (and children!), and I was out at night trying to be a stand-up comedian. It was no life for a dog. So it was a long time before I was ready. And an even longer time to find a dog-friendly apartment, and then even longer to find the right dog.

I had wanted to adopt a dog, so I began casually looking. I thought my dog would be looking for me, too—I mean, Troy had found me in his own way—but there were no dogs rushing up to me in the street, begging me to take them in, no puppies born under my porch in a storm. No cat dressed as a dog sneaking into my place. So I started looking at local rescues, the SPCA, and a few places importing dogs from LA and Mexico. It was only a matter of time before the right dog popped up.

Finally, I found him at a city pound about fifty kilometres out of the city. He was a white pit bull mix, with a brown patch over his eye. He had one leg that was longer than the others and suffered from chronic, incurable pain, but he did so with a pink tongue sticking out the side of his happy, silly face. My heart sank when I was told he would only live a year or two, but if I was open to fostering him for that time, I could have him. I took the night to consider and decided that two years of spoiling this dog was worth the heartbreak. By the time I called back the next day, a local rescue had taken him in, scheduled the operation to remove his bad leg, and planned to rehab him. A three-legged dog is good luck and a promise that I would never have to take up jogging! So I applied again to adopt this beautiful dog and waited six weeks for him to heal. During that time, the foster family fell in love with the tripod and kept him. I cried like a child. I was at once so happy for the dog and the people, and so upset that I didn't have my dog. But, really, it was for the best. He was ninety pounds of thunder on three legs at that point and staring down a long and happy life with a family with a yard. They even had a Jeep and probably laughed out loud at TV shows that I am too cool to watch (BAZINGA). Oh, how I hated them, for at least a day!

Then I pulled myself up and started to look again. Over six months I requested information on twelve dogs and applied to adopt three. Nothing worked out and I grew impatient with the conversations I was having with the rescues: The dog "only bit *one* child" or "only attacks other dogs when provoked" or, the one that worried me most, "can't be around men, he's terrified of men." I mean, hey dog, same here, but that is *my* bit! I don't need a dog to hold a mirror up to me every day! The rescue agencies often required an adoptee who worked from home, with a backyard, or insisted that the dog needed to be fed a raw food diet or revealed it wasn't housebroken and may never be, and on and on. Don't make direct eye contact with the dog, don't sing Sade around the dog, make sure your neighbours' children know how to call the dog off while protecting their faces if they accidentally move too quickly around the dog. I was unsure I would ever find a dog that would fit my life, and I theirs.

Annoyed by my constant complaining, my friend Warren suggested I buy a dog. I said no. HOW DARE HE? I AM GOING TO RESCUE, AND BE RESCUED BY, A DOG, AND SAY AS MUCH ON SOCIAL MEDIA. I am going to hashtag the shit out of my selfless act of adopting a dog #adoptdontshop! Then he suggested he buy me a dog, and I was like, maybe? I do love a bargain.

So I said fuck it and started looking at dog breeders. I became a part-time dog breeder investigator, piecing together websites that led me to large breeding facilities instead of what was advertised (small home breeders), until I found a few options for miniature poodles, and from there, I found Susan and sent her an email. A day later, she contacted me, and we began what felt like a seventeen-part interview process. The first was a forty-five-minute phone conversation where she made sure I wasn't a weirdo. After the first visit to her home, where I met seven hysterical miniature poodles with almost no rules, I was put on the waiting list for a puppy. The stud dog that would be the "dad" of my puppy was spring-loaded, and before me was a ballet of black curls and pipe-cleaner legs. I had only ever met one miniature poodle, named Django, who was smart and calm and seemed to think people were annoying. Django, people are annoying, GOOD BOY! I hadn't researched the breed much. I read that poodles were in the top two most intelligent dog breeds, easily trained, and very sensitive, often bonding with just one family member. Since there is only one person in my family (me), this seemed good. He would have no other choice but to bond with me, how perfect? I missed the part about them being hunting dogs but would learn that later.

Months passed and no puppy. No word from the breeder, either. On the day I followed up, the breeder said that one of her dogs was expecting. I asked for a male dog, I guess because I'd already had male dogs and heard they house-train a bit faster. I waited for the dog to give birth and hoped my puppy would be in that litter. I felt horrible that I was part of this process. Buying and selling dogs was a far cry from scanning adoption sites, and now I was letting go of the idea of myself as a person who rescues a helpless dog and settling on being a cruel and unforgivable jerk who just gives up and buys a perfect dog.

Finally, two puppies were born. Just two. One male and one female. The breeder kept one female puppy from every litter to breed and show at dog shows. The male could be mine if I wanted him. I did. The breeder sent me a picture of him being weighed on a scale inside of a shoe. He was so small. My friend and I drove out to the burbs and met my puppy. I held my dog and wondered what I was getting into. He was warm, his fur like a lambskin coat, his breath milky.

In December I went to pick the dog up, and I named him Hank. The breeder seemed hesitant when I arrived. I was tired after a long year of general life and work, and looking for a puppy was really not what I had planned. I felt weighed down by this choice and the burden of constantly trying to convince the breeder I was going to be a good dog owner. Her hesitation felt like another emotional obstacle I had to drag my will over.

When I managed to reword, "What now, lady?" she said, "Well, I was thinking that maybe you might want to wait for another puppy. In the twenty years I have been breeding poodles, I have only had one other dog like this, and he was a lot of trouble. He was the only puppy that was ever sent back to me, and Hank is just like him."

Um, what the fuck is going on here? I thought. *He's a puppy.* Hank looked up at me, and I looked down at him. Then he bit his sister and looked back up at me.

"How can you tell?" I asked.

"Well, he never puts his tail down, ever. He's very bossy. He will be very stubborn and defiant. He won't be an easy dog."

All this from a tail? Quick, look at my palms: When will I die? This dog? This four-pound bird-boned lump? I trusted that she could tell a lot about a dog, and she tried to match a dog's personality to the person buying the dog, and she saw a red flag when matching us. But to be honest, he sounded just like me, and I am great!

I looked over at Hank's sister, who was whining for attention, whose tail seemed to go both up and down, and I looked at Hank, who was still staring at me, tail up, silent. The breeder assured me she would totally understand if I didn't want to take Hank, and I could have the first male puppy that was born next. But I was taking Hank. Because who else would? He didn't ask to be here. I started this whole thing. And I related to him. I am not easy to get along with, I am stubborn, I want things to go my way, always. And I don't give up on dogs, or people, for those reasons. What if he ended up with a family who didn't understand him? What if someone abandoned him or hurt him? Something cracked inside me and I remembered another dog, one I didn't have for long when I was a child, a dog named Charlie, who was difficult and was put to sleep when I was at school one day. Nope. I knew that Hank was my dog, and somehow, fate, and quite a bit of money, had brought us together. As well as a few rides from friends, because I can't drive. Oh, and the constant rejection of life.

So Hank came home with me that night, tucked into my winter coat, his warm milk belly cradled in my palm on the long drive back into the city. I had taken two weeks off work to "bond" with him.

When Hank got home to my small puppy-proofed apartment, I had everything I thought I needed to keep a puppy safe and happy. He waddled over to the Christmas tree and pulled on the plug. Okay, so no Christmas lights. Then he peed on the tree skirt. That's fine, no tree skirt. Then he pooped in his crate and got poop all over himself and started to scream. I wanted to scream, too. He was so upset. Until this moment he'd had a mother to clean him. I gave him a bath in the tiny bathroom sink, which made him cry louder, and dried him with the hair dryer. He quieted down. A dog who likes a hair dryer? Weird. I wrapped him up in a towel and watched him sleep. He was so helpless and alone. No dog mother or sister. The little comfort he knew was gone. Part of the process of training a dog is this practice of taking them away from their family so young. I knew so much about dogs, but I realized I knew nothing about puppies. I felt so sorry for him.

The next two weeks were about me trying to keep both of us alive. I caught the flu and don't remember anything but both of us crying a lot. He peed, he bit me, he played non-stop. I coughed, I tried to sleep when he slept, and I thought about how if I died from the flu, who would take care of this crazy puppy? Did you know that puppies don't know how to go for a walk? They don't. You have to train a puppy to walk. And it is a slow and frustrating process. I would wake up three or four times a night to his crying to be let out, and then stand in the cold, wet night, waiting for him to pee or poop, only to get back inside and he would need to go again. I had imagined all of my great dog skills would translate to being great with Hank. That we would bond instantly. That he would like me. He didn't. When they are puppies is the only time I think a dog is truly like a wolf, truly wild. They have no idea that they were bred from something wolflike thousands of years ago into a small, floppy, silly dog. The scariest part was how small and fragile he was. I had always had big dogs, and this one looked like a ball of yarn.

As the months wore on, my life changed. I got used to waking up to Hank's cries to go outside in the middle of the night. My hands were red and chapped and scraped from Hank's needle-like puppy teeth. My clothes were covered in drops of poodle pee. I gave up my one rule to never go outside in my pajamas to seemingly *only* go outside in my pajamas. Hank was expensive, and pretty unlikable. He never stopped moving except to sleep. I was bested by his energy and started to call him the Wig with Teeth or Hank the Shape. He was impossible to photograph, impossible to tame. I did everything I read I was supposed to do and, still, he was wild and sharp. It seemed like every other week we were at the vet for eye infections (he had three in his first few months, his tiny beady eyes caked shut with green crust I would gently wash away before carefully putting drops in), ear infections, weird poops, or expensive checkups. The vet said the difference between having a puppy and having a baby is that we have no biological imperative to keep a puppy alive. Hank, overall, felt like a mistake.

But slowly, I started to figure him out. He was smart. Well, he was dog smart. He learned to sit in a few minutes, he was house-trained in a day or two, but everything else was a mystery. He didn't walk; he jumped, or pranced, and rarely were all four feet on the floor. Each day was a race against Hank's energy in an effort for both of us to sleep. I put him to bed every night in his crate and hoped the next day would be better.

Finally, Hank started to walk with some purpose. If I could just get him to walk, I might have a chance at tiring him out. I signed us up for puppy class (where Hank was the silliest dog in the bunch and not the youngest by a long shot) and had a trainer teach him to listen to basic commands and help me correct my mistakes. One night, after looking over at him staring at me through the gate in his crate, I decided that maybe Hank would be a better dog if he could sleep on the bed, and for the first time, he slept through the night. My heart rate slowed. Hank's heart rate slowed. He moved up the bed and nestled under my arm. He started sleeping curled up beside me, and I learned that Hank was the sweetest dog, and unlike any dog I'd had: he was a snuggler.

One morning, when Hank was about nine months old, he woke up with a limp. His little left back foot was cramped. He wouldn't let me touch his back. The vet couldn't figure out what it was. The first round of X-rays showed no damage. We tried physio, cold laser therapy, and pain medication, but each day it got worse and worse. He would scream in pain when he tried to jump or play, and soon his other hind leg was giving out, too. He would scoot painfully over to me, collapse at my feet, and lean against me for comfort. And the fact that he was just nine months old exacerbated the problem. He couldn't get better if he couldn't stop moving. I was told to carry him uphill or downhill, and up and down the two flights of stairs to my apartment. No jumping, no running, no playing. So basically, no poodling. I biked home from work almost every day at lunch to carry his little body down to the front yard to pee and then back up the stairs. I ate lunch at my desk, if I could afford lunch that day, as Hank's vet bills were mounting and, still, no one really knew what was wrong.

The vet suggested a few options after a series of treatments, another round of X-rays, and wild guesses led to no improvement. With Hank only getting worse, I chose the most in-depth and expensive option. I couldn't keep him in pain like this much longer. We went to see the Canadian specialist for lameness, who worked up in the mountains, a visit that cost $1,300. And we finally had an answer. Hank had torn not one but both of his psoas muscles, the muscles that hold the pelvis to the spine. He would get better, but it would be slow, painful, and expensive. His treatments were only available at a vet 100 kilometres outside the city. But a person does what they have to do for their family. I spent all my vacation days taking Hank to vet appointments, all my lunch breaks checking on him, and all my days and most of my sleepless nights watching over him. He had no appetite, he lost weight, and I would lie on the floor hand-feeding him anything he would eat that day: cheese, a bit of meat. He would have a good day, perhaps only limping when he woke up and after a bit of exercise, and I would feel hopeful, but soon his back end would droop again. My friends Abby and Graham took turns letting him out at lunch so I could spare myself a day of biking in the summer heat, and they would patiently respond to my numerous hysterical text messages asking *How was his limp?* and *Did he pee?* He was always cared for by my village of dear friends.

When he didn't improve, I started living on the floor with him: I took my bed frame apart and pulled the mattress onto the floor, covered the couch with chairs so neither of us could jump on it. My arm started to hurt from carrying him, but I still lifted him up whenever he needed it, to see a bird or bark at a cat, to be part of the world a bit more. I sat on the lawn with him so he could watch people for hours. I tried to keep him engaged and calm. I tried to stay calm and present, too, always mindful that his needs came first, that he was my responsibility, so I better do my best for him, no matter what. The hardest part was that he couldn't play with other dogs. He just had me, and I tried to mimic puppy play as best I could, but I was no substitute.

Our neighbours started to stop by and sit with Hank. He had kept them laughing so hard in the drizzling Vancouver winter that his recovery meant something to them, too. They offered to make meals or visit, but I was already accepting so much from my friends, family, and co-workers that I knew I could never pay back. It was a lonely time for me. One day someone saw me walking with Hank in my arms and said, "Dogs are meant to walk," and I started screaming, "HE CAN'T FUCKING WALK AND WHEN HE TRIES, IT COSTS ME HUNDREDS OF DOLLARS." As soon as they were out of sight I broke down and sobbed. We were on month three of vet visits and Hank was no better. I started to wonder if he would ever get better.

But we kept going. After a few more months, his right leg was almost normal, but his left was a shadow. Thin, floppy, and often tucked into his body. Yet Hank was still the same: full of life. The last of his puppy teeth were falling out, and he was turning soft and sweet. He was becoming a dog.

The long trips up to Squamish to see the specialist were so hard on Hank. He was terrified of the treatments, for which he was muzzled and manipulated, pulled and poked with acupuncture needles. Both of us exhausted, we would get a ride back into the city from a friend, and I would hope pet insurance would cover one more visit. Each visit to a vet came with the anxiety that perhaps he would never heal, and I would have to face putting him down. We went to physio each week as well. One week there would be slight improvement but nothing the next. Hank had a CAT scan, and we learned that if the treatment we were already doing didn't pay off, there wasn't anything else we could do (dogs and CAT scans, am I right?). It seemed time to double down. I wasn't losing Hank.

It took a full year and an unknown-because-I-can't-bear-to-look amount of money for Hank to heal. I definitely could have bought, like, my dream couch, or a really shitty car, or paid off that loan I took out for the hot-dog stand I never followed through on. It was going to be called So Long Hot Dog, and I was only going to serve foot-long hot dogs. Anyway, in that time, Hank the Shape, the Wig with Teeth, finally started to walk without pain. His left leg took another four months to rebuild muscle and still curves a bit. Neighbours stop to point out how well he is walking and what a good job I did with him. I try not to cry. My left shoulder is frozen and will be for two years. Now I go to physio each week, and the irony is not lost on me.

Sometimes, at night, I wake up to Hank howling in his sleep, his small face turned skyward and his plaintive primal cry speaking to an unknowable dream. I reach down and touch this small soul, and I am thankful for the comfort he brings me each day. What a privilege it is to own a dog.

And I am thankful that Hank does not eat diapers.

PHOTO: Tanya Goehring

ALICIA TOBIN is a comedian and writer living and working in Vancouver. She loves baked goods, animals, friendship, and her miniature poodle, Hank Tobin. On any given day you can find Alicia trying to get through a combination of taking on too much to get around to and doing nothing. *So You're a Little Sad, So What?* is her first book.